Praise for
CLUTTERFREE **REVOLUTION**

"Evan inspires a new generation of conscious consumers. A must read for every household in America."

– Casey Sheahan | former President & CEO, Patagonia, Inc.

"*ClutterFree Revolution* does more than demystify the complexity of our stuff. It guides us through an honest conversation about what matters most. Evan shows us how the power of intentional simplicity can transform ourselves and help change the world."

– Dr. Melva Green | expert psychiatrist from the critically acclaimed TV series *Hoarders: Family Secrets*

"Honest and inspiring, *ClutterFree Revolution* transcends the process of designing soulful spaces into an empowering movement. Evan reminds us to think beyond our own homes and recommit to the global solution. *ClutterFree Revolution* delivers with heart."

– Xorin Balbes | author of *SoulSpace* & founder of the world renowned design firm, TempleHome

"Elegant. An adjective, meaning pleasingly ingenious and simple. If you'd like your life to have more of it and more of the richness and fulfillment that comes with it, then I strongly recommend you read *ClutterFree Revolution*. Apply its sage-like and practical wisdom, and watch your life soar on the wings of new possibility."

– Rod Stryker | American yoga master & author of *The Four Desires: Creating a Life of Purpose, Happiness, Prosperity and Freedom*

"Your clutter is your autobiography. The sooner you read *Clutter-Free Revolution*, the faster you will reach your goals—inside and out. I highly recommend this book."

– Dr. Brian Alman | bestselling author of *The Voice* and *Less Stress for Kids*

"We all have the responsibility to shape public policy and advance issues of social justice. Of course, advocacy requires activism in the public sphere, but what is equally essential is focused activism in our personal lives. *ClutterFree Revolution* is a hard-hitting guide to thriving with less. Evan's Revolution sets the stage for empowering communities around day-to-day practice. Read it and use it."

– Dedrick Asante-Muhammad | former Senior Director Economic Department, NAACP

"We are inherently spiritual beings, but many of us have lost sight of the deeply meaningful connection we have with one another. Amidst our things, we've lost a bit of ourselves. *ClutterFree Revolution* illuminates the inspiring journey home."

– Lexie Potamkin | human rights activist & author of the *What is Spirit* book series

"If we are to empower the next generation of conscious leaders, we must focus on what matters most—and that starts at home. *ClutterFree Revolution* is about so much more than tidying up...it is a rally cry for Americans to get back in the game. Evan joins the ranks of today's brightest and most compelling champions of 'Conscious Leadership.' *ClutterFree Revolution* is a must read for anyone serious about transforming their life!"

– Mark Hoog | nationally acclaimed motivational speaker, founder of the Children's Leadership Institute & author of the bestselling *Growing Field* book series

"It's only when we live simply, that we can experience clarity. And we must have clarity, to be able to serve fully. If that is your desire, then this is your book."

– Steve Burnett | author of *How to Double Your Business Without Making a Sale*

CLUTTER FREE
REVOLUTION

SIMPLIFY YOUR
STUFF
ORGANIZE YOUR
LIFE
& SAVE THE
WORLD

EVAN MICHAEL ZISLIS

JUNIPER PRESS

JUNIPER PRESS

Juniper Press, First Edition 2015

DISCLAIMER
This book covers a practical and accessible means of dealing with the complexities of life and material possessions. It is not a substitute for legal, financial, or medical advice; nor counseling, therapy, or other social, emotional, behavioral or mental health interventions. The author has vetted the Intentional Solutions 3-Step Method with countless clients, however does not guarantee specific results.

Cover Design: Paul Thomas - LightNowMedia.com
Book Layout and Design: Paul Thomas - Light Now Media
Editing: Kate Makled
Author's photo courtesy of RebeccaStumpf.com
Back cover photo courtesy of RebeccaStumpf.com

Library of Congress Control Number: 2015910813

eBook ISBN 978-1-942646-18-1
Print ISBN 978-0-692-48168-4

Published and printed in the United States of America

10 9 8 7 6 5 4 3 2 1

For Juno,

It is my absolute delight and charge in life to help guide and shelter you, nurture and adore you—forever. Together, we will enjoy tender triumphs and endure heroic disappointment. There will be untold sadness and indescribable joy. In every single moment, my heart will burst with love and pride for the beautiful miracle you are. My mistakes will be many, but no matter what grief, embarrassment, or headache I may cause you, my only intention is steadfast and simple: to protect you from harm and guide you in a direction of peace and happiness.

Know that you have been my greatest teacher, my most treasured friend, and my single-most rewarding endeavor. My love for you fills my heart with endless happiness, and to you I dedicate this book—and my life.

Wishing you love and abundance,
   – *Daddy*

CONTENTS

CLUTTER FREE
REVOLUTION

As any Hoarders fan might tell you, I will always be honest,
because without honesty, transformation is not possible.
– Dr. Melva Green

FOREWORD

by Dr. Melva Green

Bless your clutter! That's right – bless it! This work is not about *getting rid* of our clutter. *Life* is clutter. Every day is a gift, presented to us with an infinite variety of miraculous (and messy) choices. Each and every day invites us to choose, "What will be important to me? What will be important to my life? What will help me to thrive? What will help me to feel connected to my humanity—and to my Source?"

This work is about embracing an empowering understanding of our past—that propels us towards a more promising future. The *things* that create clutter all around us are an opportunity to bring intention to what really matters. Each and every item that stands in the way between hope and the life we seek is an opportunity for spiritual growth. Let us rise to the occasion and choose with thoughtful intention.

Our clutter, after all, is merely the physical manifestation of our emotional turmoil and our anxieties about our belief systems. What a blessing—to be presented with a tangible process for making peace within ourselves, with our families, and with our legacy. When forced to confront these powerfully impactful questions, we are not simply clearing the excess from our spaces—we are *evolving* as interconnected spiritual beings. Let us not be *rid* of our clutter—let us celebrate this process.

Our clutter forces us to ask, "What is this here to teach me? How is this here to help transform my life? How is this here to connect me to my ancestry? How will this help me to experience love more authentically—and connect more deeply with those I cherish most?" These questions help us to frame our understanding of clutter in a way that promotes gratitude, discovery, compassion, curiosity, and self-acceptance. These questions help us to form a more meaningful identity of who we are—and *why*.

The benefits of answering these questions and seeing them through with conviction, absolutely helps us to manifest our limitless potential. When we serve our highest good, we become available to those who look to us for guidance and direction. After all, how can we show up for those who depend on us, when we have not given ourselves permission to care *for ourselves*? This work is about prioritizing and choosing that which supports our highest good—in support of those we mean to honor and serve, *including* ourselves.

When Evan first asked me to endorse *ClutterFree Revolution*, I was taken aback by his heartfelt approach to both his method and *why* this work is so important. My work as a board certified psychiatrist and spiritual healer marries both Western medicine with traditional practices rooted in the ancestry of humanity. As a medical doctor, I have advised countless individuals through their struggle to understand their connection to what is deeply valued. My "real-life" healing practice and my work on the Lifetime television series *Hoarders: Family Secrets* has been a fantastically wild ride, and a profoundly humbling experience. That said, Evan absolutely gets it.

In light of my life's work, I am delighted to share Evan's inspiring message with the world. His process reminds us what matters most and invites us to affirm for ourselves, to our families, to the world—and to our Creator, "Yes! *This* is what matters. *This* is what is meaningful to me. *This* is what I am here for." What a tremendous gift—and how timely. We need Evan's Revolution now more than ever, and I am sincerely hopeful that his book may, indeed, help save the world.

As we embark on the *ClutterFree Revolution* together, I leave you with this. My friends, please remember compassion. Let go of perfection, unless used to describe where we are in this moment. Our divinity lies in our willingness to embrace the promise of who we seek to become—and in our humble pursuit of that vision. We are all worthy of loving-kindness, forgiveness, and radical self-acceptance. And so, as we look deeper within—I invite you to do so with compassion, gratitude and a resounding sense of abundance for today.

Having completed a psychiatry residency at Johns Hopkins University School of Medicine, Dr. Melva Green, MD, MBA, MPH is board certified and widely regarded as one of America's top psychiatrists. Best known for her work on the popular and critically acclaimed Lifetime television series *Hoarders: Family Secrets*, Dr. Green is the co-author of *Breathing Room: Open Your Heart by Decluttering Your Home*.

ACKNOWLEDGEMENTS

I think life is a bit like playing soccer when you're five. There's stuff happening all around us, but nobody's really sure what to do—so, invariably we end up picking flowers, walking in circles and racing to kick the ball once in a while. From time to time, we get lucky and punt it in the right direction, but usually we're just kind of looking around—wondering what the hell everyone is yelling about.

As an adult, I still find life awfully confusing—so I try to keep it simple.

I learned the virtues of simplicity from my family, who mostly seem to prefer keeping everything magnificently complicated. We always had fun, and looking back there were a few near misses, but no *actual* disasters. With all due respect, life with my ruthlessly entertaining family has been a series of hilarious capers, astonishing misadventures, and epic cluster-fucks. Their approach to everything is riotously—elaborate.

Let me clarify. I adore my family. My mom is the most committed and enthusiastic person to have ever lived. My dad is the funniest, most generous and most dedicated guy I know. My little (older) sister is without a doubt, the smartest and hardest working individual on the planet. Together, they represent the accumulation of traits I admire (and seem to lack) most. C'est la vie.

I thank my mom for teaching me humility and kindness. I thank my dad for teaching me integrity and generosity. I thank my little (older) sister for teaching me perseverance and etiquette. I am who I am today because of the spectacular adventures I've shared with them, and I would not trade a single moment of the life they've gifted to me. For you, I am grateful beyond comprehension or description. In fact, my head hurts just thinking about it.

I thank my beautiful wife for her endless love and support. She is the brightest star of my life and I just seem to fall more deeply in love with her every time she walks in the room. On the coldest days of the year, her light is the only warmth I need—and my heart is eternally full with yumminess and gratitude that she chose me. To her I pledge my heart, my love, and my life—for at least 57 years of marriage.

I thank my daughter, Juniper, for teaching me more about myself than anyone ever could. Like your namesake, you are a powerfully resilient and infinitely strong little being—with so much life in you, you can hardly sit still. My heart is split wide open with the pride I feel that I belong to you, and I consider it the greatest honor of my life to know you and hear the words, "I love you, Daddy" spoken from your lips. To you, I dedicate this, my first book—and all the days of my life. You are the only legacy that matters to me; you are the sole inspiration for my being, my attempt to make the world a better place, and my misguided urgency for safety. My sweet baby girl, I wish you a lifetime of peace, love, adventure, and abundance.

Special thanks to Dr. Melva Green, Casey Sheahan, Rod Stryker, Xorin Balbes, Dr. Brian Alman, Dedrick Asante-Muhammud, Lexie Potamkin, Mark Hoog, Steve Burnett and so many others who enthusiastically endorsed *ClutterFree Revolution*. Thank you for believing in me. I am grateful beyond words.

To Paul Thomas and Heather Mandel at www.LightNowMedia.com, thank you for your generous guidance, expertise and friendship. To masterminds Emily Hightower (www.Ondalu.com) and Elinor Fish (www.ElinorFish.com), I thank you for your friendship, wisdom and inspiration.

Much gratitude and respect to extraordinary friends, family, and mentors from around the world. LOVE & ABUNDANCE to all of you.

INTRODUCTION

HOPE

Hope lived for fairy tale happy endings, sentimental gestures, and the romance of epic love. At forty-two, she'd outgrown the naiveté of her youth. She'd completed an art degree, traveled the world, learned to cook, started a career, saved a little money, and became close friends with several interesting people. She'd enjoyed a few lovers, wrote in her journal, and lost her mother to cancer. Hope grew up, but never out of touch with the sentimental side of her that longed for a meaningful, deeply fulfilling life.

Now married fourteen years to a kind man with a passion for brunch buffets, vintage comic books, and hot stock tips, they lived happily with their three active children in a comfortable home on the edge of town. Like most of her friends, Hope was mostly preoccupied with the business of running a household and raising a family. Caught up in the momentum that had become her life, Hope embodied the American dream—and yet, just beneath the surface, she felt something had been lost along the way. The inertia of her life just felt impossibly cluttered, relentlessly chaotic, and hopelessly disconnected from the fantastic visions of her youth. And yet, there seemed no easy way to make the sweeping changes she craved.

Feeling guilty about the absurdity of it, from time to time she would daydream about getting her own place—something straight out of the pages of *Dwell* magazine, sparsely furnished and bathed in light. Perhaps a refurbished loft near a quiet bistro, a pristine retreat with an expansive writing desk. Hope fantasized about an organized art studio, an immaculate kitchen and an organic vegetable garden on a balcony with spectacular views. She dreamt of slipping out of her luxurious pillow-top bed, uninterrupted, into a hot bath, losing herself in a library of romance novels, restorative yoga and perfect cups of freshly brewed craft coffee. Locked away in the uplifting music box of her mind, she nourished this expansive, pristine space without the chaos and clutter her life had become.

Dear Evan,

If I understand correctly, you help people with clutter problems. After several years in denial, I think I may need some help. I have three children with a lot of stuff. My husband is an avid collector. Our home is comfortable, but our things have taken over the whole house. I am tired of tidying up all the time yet getting nowhere. I'm embarrassed to say we don't really have guests over anymore because the house is always a mess. We've talked about moving into a larger home, but we are upside down with our current mortgage, and I'm not sure how realistic that is. I could use some help with our clutter and getting on top of our bills. I put my career on hold when our youngest was born, so I'd also like to create a home office where I can start thinking about getting back to work. If this sounds like something you can help me with, I'd like to learn more about your process and discuss next steps.

Hopelessly cluttered,

Hope

Dear Hope,

Thank you for reaching out. First, let me say how much I admire your courage. So many people deal with the same challenges you describe, but don't reach out for help. Please don't feel bad. Despite what you may think, it's not your fault. Clutter is a pandemic. It's become part of the literal fabric of our culture. Like your husband, we have become collectors of *things*. The conveyor belt of new things coming in the front door is as much as ten times the amount we get rid of out the back door. This creates the phenomenon I call the *too much*. The volume of our *things* just becomes unmanageable.

I help people drastically increase what they get rid of, and filter the new stuff coming in the front door. Once those systems are in place, we get organized. The less stuff we bring in to our lives in the first place, the more space we have to manage and enjoy the things we love. More importantly, without all that excess, we can focus on the things that matter most: your family, your career, creating the life you *want*. Getting on top of this situation and making lasting change is easier than you think. You can do it. I can help. Let's schedule some time to talk this week.

Hopeful,

Evan

And in the end, it's not the years in your life that count. It's the life in your years.
– Abraham Lincoln

In the moments before our passing, as we look back on our lives, all that will matter is who we loved, what we did, how and why we lived. Because everything else was just *stuff*. In the course of our short, precious lifetimes, our earthly possessions should only serve to empower us in becoming who we want to be, and aid us in achieving what we want to do. The superfluous becomes irrelevant, a frivolous distraction, a liability. This book serves as a catalyst for change, a practical guide for action and a manifesto for empowering ourselves and our children with a clearer understanding of humanity's potential to thrive with *less*.

Simplicity is the ultimate sophistication.
– Leonardo Da Vinci

Simplify Your Way to a Better Life

When we occupy simple, peacefully stimulating environments, we experience enhanced sensations of calm, focus, and joy. We become more productive. Communication, social engagement and relationships flourish. We become exponentially more inspired to stay active, take on challenging activities, solve complex problems, collaborate, innovate, eat healthfully, exercise regularly, pursue and realize life goals.

In this book, I share my proven three-step method for transforming any space from agitated chaos to functional serenity. Perhaps more importantly, we'll examine the psychology behind our clutter-producing tendencies, and explore an empowering new paradigm—one that frees us from the emotionally-driven behaviors and culturally-reinforced norms that undermine our efforts to build healthier lifestyles. This book is not just a practical guide for tidying up, it's a manual for living a better life.

The Revolution Against Corporate Imperialism

This book is not simply about organizing your closets. It is a call to arms, a rally cry to take a stand in the revolution against Corporatocracy and commercial imperialism—to champion a new standard of common sense and sustainability. At its very core, the revolution starts in our homes, with our own families. For those looking to evolve out of a cluttered existence, this book is a practical guide to inform, instruct, and inspire the journey to a better life—a more rewarding, more meaningful, more intentional life of purpose and abundance.

This book is about reprioritizing, redirecting scarce resources, and developing a more sustainable paradigm of market accountability and consumer responsibility. If you are reading this, after all, you probably have more opportunity and more viable resources than three quarters of the earth's population. Paring down our stuff and becoming mindful about our spaces is not just a pleasant alternative to living in disarray, it is a moral imperative as members of the human race. How we behave as consumers has profound implications on what happens at home as well as around the globe. This book is an instruction manual for a return to intentional simplicity, a return to less *stuff* and more *life*. When we make space for what matters in life, we enjoy our lives more. We feel more inspired to realize our full potential, and we have more energy to contribute to the global solution. We cannot leave this important work to corporations who only seek to profit from our complacency.

This book is about waking up to the reality of what matters most: who we love, what we do, how and why we live. *Because everything else is just stuff.* Take this knowledge and share it with the people you love. In doing so, collectively we become empowered to clear the cluttered path to the life we seek. This is the *ClutterFree Revolution*.

PART 1

THE
BACKSTORY

Clutter is not just the stuff on your floor—it's anything that stands between you and the life you want to be living.

– Peter Walsh

1
CHOCOLATE FROSTING AND SEX TOYS

Using this book as a practical guide, you will learn to purge your junk, organize your stuff, and design spaces that inspire you to create your ideal life. Applying my simple three-step method to the stuff in your space is a springboard for understanding. Beyond spaces and places, in fact, the three-step formula serves as a metaphor and a unifying methodology for managing the figurative clutter in our lives.

In this book, you will learn to simplify, achieve clarity, and stay inspired in all areas of your life, including how you think, eat, exercise, work, play, communicate, manage your time, organize your thoughts, and implement your great ideas. I know this—not only will these simple steps work for you, they'll work for your kids, your spouse, your mother, your best friend, your next door neighbor, and strangers you will never meet living on the other side of the planet—today, tomorrow, and forever.

Intentional Solutions 3-Step Method:
Simplify. Clarify. Inspire.

There are no bells and whistles here. No fancy apps, elaborate platforms, or overproduced instructional videos. Just three steps: simplify, clarify, inspire. We'll discuss and apply these three steps over and over again for effective, long-lasting results. These steps are easy to learn, easy to remember, and easy to implement across the board, right out of the box. Most importantly, these principles are timeless and universal in their application. Three steps, strategically repeated with intentional resolve, their elegant practicality without limitation.

I Know You

I need to preface what I'm about to say with something important. This work is EXTREMELY personal. At some point in the process, a lot of people get emotional. Some cry. It's awesome, and there's a transformation that happens for them when they get clear and reconnect to life with a paradigm that supports simplicity. When I work with clients one-on-one, people can feel the sincerity of my tone, the assurance of my plan—the love in my heart.

But books can read a little impersonal, and sometimes things get lost in translation. I don't serve anyone by sounding like a know-it-all. There's no way for me to build trust if I inadvertently come across sounding arrogant and condescending. So, I want to put this out there on the front end—the passion in my message comes from sincerity and a hope for you to become inspired. The truth is—I understand what you are dealing with on a very personal level. My hope is for you to open to this process, believe in yourself, and take intentional steps on your own behalf.

So, before we begin—please know in your heart that I mean what I'm about to say; intending for you to only receive it feeling honored and respected—no matter where you are in your journey to becoming a clutter-free Zen master.

Like I know Hope, I know you. With zero judgment and all the love in my heart, please believe me when I say, I know this problem well. I'm nobody special. I'm just a regular guy. I like riding bikes with my kid, playing with my dog, watching romantic comedies with my wife, and occasionally devouring a good chocolate chip cookie. I may be just a regular guy, but I have stumbled on a foundational formula for helping people that is remarkably effective for solving problems that might otherwise appear complicated. I've been applying this ridiculously simple three-step method over and over again to help countless people simplify and organize the stuff in their spaces—and it's proven astonishingly effective. It is easier than most people think. I know it works. And I know you.

Normally, I would not presume to impose what I know (or what I think I know) on someone else. But I know YOU (or at least I think I do). I live with my family in a quiet community in the heart of the Colorado Rockies. We lead a recreational lifestyle in the mountains, *and we've got stuff.* With a five year old daughter, many hobbies, and a dog, we also have our fair share of clutter. I'm all about transparency and full disclosure, so let me reiterate—my home is not the sterile glass jar people imagine it to be.

As a second-generation Army brat, I grew up in a household with an eclectic assortment of bizarre artifacts, meticulously gathered from the far-flung places where we lived and traveled. My childhood homes were a shrine to our fervent excursions abroad. Prolific collectors of things, my family inherited and amassed heirloom treasures from every corner of the globe. Wooden, glass, stone, metallic, paper, fabric arts and crafts—and the full assortment of fragments from all manner of flora and fauna—every room of our house featured a chaotic monument of sorts, paying homage to generations of travel.

That said, I know you. Because you picked up this book, I can bet you're not unlike me, or the clients I've worked with in my professional practice. I'm the first to admit, I don't know the most important things about you. But I can say with clarity and compassionate confidence—I know your spaces, I know your stuff, and I know your clutter.

How do I know? As an organizational consultant, I actually live in clutter the majority of the time. In fact, I'm steeped in it. That is the irony of my life. The bulk of my time is spent meticulously dissecting the closets, garages, hallways, playrooms, bedrooms, living rooms, home offices, kitchens, basements, business offices, storage lockers, and other generally messy spaces of my client base. Sifting through endless piles, sorting what stays from what goes, and getting it all organized and put away with intentional precision—I am a clutter *super freak.*

Not convinced? Let's test it. I know about those jeans you'll fit into again someday. I know about your collections of shoes and stretch pants. I know about your obsession with great bags. I know you still have cassette tapes, but nothing to play them on. I know about your spring-loaded cabinets, booby-trapped with plastic yogurt containers and cheap water bottles. I know the condition of your food pantry. I bet I know what's in your garage, attic, basement, crawl space, and that storage locker across town. I know about your piles of unopened mail. I know about your peculiar collections. I know the contents of the junk drawers in your kitchen and in your desk. I know about your filing cabinet. I know the state of your kids' bedrooms, playrooms, book bags, and school lockers. I know what's in your bathroom, possibly better than you do. I know about your collection of magazines. I know about the old love letters and your box of treasures from high school. I know about the endless photo albums and odd family heirlooms. I know about your great grandma's china plates, crystal wine glasses, and the silver. I know about your piles of laundry. I know about all the little things you've been saving because you're sure they must be important—for something. I even know about the chocolate frosting, the old weed, and the sex toys. I know all the hiding places where you shove everything fifteen minutes before your guests arrive. It's okay—I love you, and *believe me, I know.*

I Also Know How You Feel

I know because *I've seen it*. I've seen your stuff—because your stuff is a whole lot like everyone else's stuff. I know sometimes you feel bad about your clutter. I know it feels overwhelming, and some days it makes you a little unhappy. I know the guilt you feel about wanting to get rid of gifts, heirlooms, and things left behind from loved ones. I know the confusion you feel about how to get rid of certain things, not sure if something is valuable, recyclable, re-usable, worth holding on to, or just plain junk. I know this process can be paralyzing. I know how easy it is to rationalize holding on to things we really don't want, like, or need. I know.

I know it can be embarrassing. I know you may not have people over as often as you'd like because you feel you're beyond "just straightening up for company." I know how isolating that can feel. I know how it feels to fall behind on your bills and rack up late fees because you haven't gone through your mail in months, or balanced your checkbook in years, if ever. I know you feel awful telling your kids to clean up their rooms when your spaces are worse than theirs. I know you overspend at the grocery store, mainly because you have absolutely no idea what's in your fridge or your pantry at home.

I know how depressing it can be. I know that feeling of isolation feeds on itself, perpetuating helplessness, despair and the kind of hopelessness that comes with inevitable defeat. I know these feelings develop into subtle thought patterns that progress into unspoken personal beliefs that advance into rationalization and justification for giving up altogether on wide swaths of your life. I know that is a slippery slope—one that leads to avoidance and destructive behaviors. I know what kind of long-term impact this can have on the health and well-being of an individual—and on the family. I know that once children normalize this environment, they inherit the conditions that keep it going, generation after generation.

I know you wish you could snap your fingers and start all over again—with a smaller place and just the handful of things you absolutely love. I'm here to tell you, YOU. CAN. *I know because I've done it myself.* I know because I've worked with countless households, businesses, students, and people in transition—from all over the world. I know that if I can—if *they* can, YOU can, too. In fact, I guarantee it. More importantly, I'll show you *how*.

As much as you love your little collections of things (shoes, jackets, bags, fill in the blank), I know you fantasize about a simple life, without all the excess. I know you only really love about twenty percent of your stuff. I know about eighty percent of your space is occupied storing the stuff you really *don't* love, and rarely, if ever, actually use. I know the psychological, emotional, physical, spiritual, intellectual, and financial impact this has on you, and on your family.

I know about the resentment you feel from tidying up. ALL. THE. TIME. I know the love-hate relationship you have with your stuff, and I know the guilt you feel around getting rid of certain things. I know about your shop therapy. I know the exhilaration you feel when you buy something new. I know the sense of euphoria you have when you walk into an immaculate hotel room for the first time, knowing it's a clean slate, a blank canvas, a clutter-free haven, *at least until you unpack.*

I'll tell you what else I know. Chronic clutter is not good for you. I know it can lead to seriously harmful conditions affecting your health and well-being, and that of your children. I know there is definitive evidence linking chronically cluttered spaces to a decrease in motivation, self-esteem, and optimism—as well as an increase in stress, anxiety, obesity, depression, substance abuse, domestic violence, social isolationism, obsessive compulsive disorders, and countless other debilitating (and often preventable) conditions.

I know there are conclusive studies showing that kids who grow up in chronically cluttered spaces are exponentially more likely to live in persistent clutter as adults. I know there is wide consensus among the medical community, affirming that the part of the brain that manages executive function, specifically creative problem-solving and complex thought, is significantly less effective in chronically cluttered environments.

Even though this may sound like you, I know this: IT'S. NOT. YOUR. FAULT. So, stop feeling guilty. Stop feeling ashamed. Stop being embarrassed. That no longer serves you. I know that YOU and the people you love have the potential to live a much healthier, much more rewarding, much more fulfilling life—a life free of the *too much*. And I know getting there is easier than you think.

Intentional Solutions is the real deal! Evan's practical strategies have transformed my home, my business, and my life. You won't find comprehensive services this good anywhere. The best investment I've made. – Denise Latousek

Out of clutter, find simplicity. From discord, find harmony. In the middle of difficulty lies opportunity.

– Albert Einstein

2
THE BIG LIE

Dear Evan,

Thank you. There is an isolation that happens when the walls seem to be coming in all around you; it's a stifling feeling that drains me. It's good to hear I'm not alone and that there is hope for the hopeless. In working with you, I've started thinking about the kinds of things we bring home. Most of it is really stuff we don't need. That alone is a breakthrough. Walking from room to room, I took your recommendation and did a quick mental inventory of the stuff in our home. I was shocked to find so much of it is just *junk*—stuff I don't ever remember needing or wanting, stuff we never should have brought home, stuff we should have gotten rid of a long time ago. I'm starting to see things from a new lens, and I can't believe how much I want to get rid of *today*. As overwhelming as this project seems now, this is the most energized I've felt in a long time.

Hopeful,

Hope

Dear Hope,

I can hear a revitalized energy in your voice and it's awesome. Congratulations! There is a shift where people begin to see their stuff in a new light, and realize how much of it they no longer want. Sometimes it's gradual, but for most people it happens all at once. They start to question why they have a thing, and then suddenly, almost everything is questioned—they decide so much of it is just a hindrance, a burden, a weight they will no longer carry. I call this the "tipping point" and it is one of the most liberating moments of realization I know. When people get there, what follows is truly an extraordinary transformation.

Consider this: **a thing should only support who you want to be and what you want to do. It should inspire you, beautify your space, or serve some useful purpose to justify its existence in your life—or it goes away forever**. Don't worry, I'll talk you through these steps one by one.

For now, begin screening the new things coming in on the "conveyor belt" at your front door. As much as possible, scrutinize every little thing to determine if it supports who you want to be and what you want to do. If it doesn't, it shouldn't even cross your threshold. Don't allow yourself or your family to inadvertently sabotage the process by getting sucked into what's trendy on television, or popular with your friends. 99.99% of that stuff is just noise—the root of the problem. Helping your family to filter what comes in will be the first paradigm shift that changes everything.

Here's a homework assignment: Actively raise your awareness to the manipulative influence commercialism has on you and your family. Notice how much that influence drives the culture of your household, and see what comes up for you around those norms as they relate to your stuff. You're doing great. Keep going!

Talk soon,

Evan

Trying to be happy by accumulating possessions is like trying to satisfy hunger by taping sandwiches all over your body.
– George Carlin

The Great Con of Our Time

How did we let things get so out of control? It was no accident. After World War II, we were told that happiness comes with the new and the *more*. When it didn't, we kept shopping; we kept spending; we kept collecting things to fill the void, sold by those committed to selling the lie. Over time, we lost sight of what makes us human beings. Our attention shifted to becoming voracious consumers.

It's evident that we have been suckered into a big lie. Strategically engineered by a small handful of sophisticated entrepreneurs, this lie is squarely focused on getting filthy rich by selling *more*. Creating our appetites for more junk, more junk *food*, more violent video games, more sexually demoralizing garbage, more toxic plastic thingies, more *everything*. With the hopes of cashing in on the sensational illusion of empty promises, we bought their lies for generations, frantically seeking happiness with every purchase.

When happiness didn't come, we bought more. And more. And more. Until one day we looked up and realized, we had inadvertently misallocated our precious resources on things that diverted our attention from what truly mattered most. One day, it seemed, our *things* had taken over our lives, and the *joy* that had been promised all along was nowhere in sight. In its place, a strange emptiness settled in, as we sat, inescapably submerged in a sea of *stuff*.

Today, we are relentlessly bombarded with commercial images of the so-called "good life." Present-day commercial advertisements are created with precise psychological insight and tested with focus groups of representative consumers. Ad agencies are masters at seduction, manipulation, and enrolling loyal followers. Because we have been deliberately trained to *believe what we are told*, we assume that whatever is for sale must be *good*—and that our very happiness *depends* on consuming that thing. It's a sick premise and a lie, but effective nonetheless. Don't believe it? Just look at us.

Think about the bizarre *things* we buy: push-up bras, gruesome video games, hairspray, battery-operated urinating dolls, high-fructose corn syrup-filled energy drinks, GMO-laden cheese puffs, plastic-wrapped war toys, and designer bins to hold it all. Seriously? We lap up whatever is put in front of us, desperately clinging to the fantastic notion that these things are intrinsically good, and may deliver us to some enchanted clutter-utopia. We actually *fight* over this ridiculous drivel in supermarkets, mega-malls, and shopping centers across the country. In pursuit of a better "deal," we line up outside stores in the wee hours for opening doorbuster sales and big product launches. At least a few times a year in this country, some melee or stampede ensues, where people are injured or killed in pursuit of more *stuff*. Individually and collectively, we have been recruited into an elaborate, deceitful scam, strategically plotted by a relatively small number of highly skilled, obscenely wealthy con artists.

The con goes something like this:

Give us your money and we'll deliver your happiness in the form of this *thing*. We'll distract you from the most important, the most beautiful, and the most urgent parts of your life—so you can obsess over the synthetic and fleeting joy inherent in whatever we're selling today. This *thing* is designed to last about thirty-seven seconds, so that empty feeling you get thirty-nine seconds from now, is easily replaced by purchasing this newly improved, superficially updated version, now available for more money.

You're not beautiful without this thing; in fact, you're probably grotesquely offensive—right up *until the moment you give us your money.* You are intrinsically unable to enjoy your life, daft as you are—*right up until the moment you give us your money.* You're not sexy and people don't like you, in fact, they are probably repulsed by you—*right up until the moment you give us your money.* The stuff you have (even if it's the stuff you bought from us yesterday or last week) is inadequate, embarrassing, and unconditionally old-fashioned. Whatever joy you feel is not the authentic kind; it's meaningless—*right up until you give us your money.* In exchange for whatever horseshit we're selling, you can go ahead and feel good about yourself for the rest of today.

The truth is, we've been suckered into the big lie. Some of us more so than others, but by and large, in our culture we've taken the bait and now we're just swallowing every glistening, empty hook dangled in front of us. The saddest part of this whole ridiculous reality—we know it. We've abandoned reason, logic, instinct, and every practical impulse to expose the truth—in exchange for something new and shiny for sale. As a result, we misspend our precious time, energy, and resources on trivial baubles, sensational sexiness, zombie-themed entertainment, and junk food. We've stopped thinking, we've stopped caring, we've stopped taking purposeful action on our own behalf. And it's killing us, both figuratively and literally.

The ClutterFree Revolution

There is a revolution stirring, a movement to return to simplicity, liberated from the fleeting, superficial glee and overdependence of gross materialism. We see it in the minimalist movement, the tiny home movement, the artistic upcycling movement, the occupy movement of the 99%, the organic movement, the conscious consumer movement, and the forward-thinking conservationist movement determined to safeguard the health and sustainability of our planet.

We know our time here is short. A mere breath and we are gone, a fleeting memory to those we leave behind. My work with clients is about empowering people to live rich, meaningful, infinitely rewarding lives, squarely focused on what matters most: who we love, what we do, how and why we live. *Because everything else is just stuff.*

I didn't always know. And it didn't just come to me like a flash in the night. My dad was an Army pathologist, so when I was a kid, my family moved a lot. As a globetrotting military brat, I learned to pack my stuff, unpack half-way around the world, get settled, re-organized, and do it all over again every twenty minutes or so. From an early age, I learned the virtues of simplicity. The experiences of my youth would help frame what I've come to understand as an adult.

Today, I believe the intentional absence of excess creates the tangible space for abundance. I believe too much can become a liability, a suffocating, toxic burden. I believe authentic happiness, and real abundance comes not from our earthly possessions, but from the fundamentals that make us uniquely human, such as:

- our meaningful connections with others,

- nurturing inspired opportunities for creativity, innovation, and intentional action, and

- the personal growth and development that comes from a life well-lived.

Clearing away the excess whittles life down to its bare essence, revealing purity of heart, integrity of character, and inspiration of purpose. When we simplify our stuff, when we get organized, when we scrutinize the stuff in our spaces with strategic intention—we become inspired to flourish, *unencumbered*.

Recommended Resources:

Life at Home in the Twenty-First Century: 32 Families Open Their Doors. Arnold, Graesch, Ragazzini, and Ochs. © 2012 UCLA CIOA Press.

After hearing great things about Evan's business for several months, I finally asked him to help me with a few organizational challenges in my home. In one meeting, Evan gave me the tools and inspiration to tackle the nagging projects and clutter. He was highly efficient, knowledgeable and thoughtful as we dove into each project during his subsequent visits. I highly recommend Evan and Intentional Solutions to anyone who needs help purging, organizing, and/or systemizing your home or business. With Evan's guidance and help, I have a much more relaxing and peaceful home. – Beth Shoemaker

There is no passion to be found playing small—in settling for a life that is less than the one you are capable of living.

– Nelson Mandela

3

INTENTIONAL ABUNDANCE

We begin with a definition and an important question.

Abundance, n.: *A joyful sense of gratitude from having that which is needed, when it is needed.*

What if the intentional absence of excess creates the tangible space for abundance?

Dear Evan,

I recently brought up the topic of abundance with my family at the dinner table. We discussed what abundance meant to each of us, and whether or not we felt a sense of abundance in our lives. After a little discussion, I asked my kids to tell me what abundance meant to *them*. I wanted to share with you their thoughts on the meaning of the word. My youngest (who is four years old) said, "I love my babies" (aka, her dolls). My middle child (seven years old) said, "I have yummy food to eat when I'm hungry." My oldest (nine years old) said simply, "We have whatever we need." My husband said, "We have more than enough."

I was struck by the gratitude in their tone, even *wisdom* in their understanding of what is available to us. So often, we take for granted what is accessible, and become complacent in how our daily needs are met. So much of our lifestyle is based on wanting more, hunting and seeking the things we don't have—just to add to the piles already in our possession. But in those few moments around our dinner table, we all agreed how grateful we are for what we have—and acknowledged how little we actually need: food, a warm place to sleep, comfortable clothes on our backs, the handful of items that give us pleasure, good health, and each other. So much of it is just stuff, excess. As a symbol of understanding, we all agreed to donate at least a few pairs of shoes to our local homeless shelter. We have so many pairs we no longer wear—and surely there must be people walking around barefoot. Thank you for inspiring me to initiate this conversation. It has truly helped shift our appreciation for less, and inspired intentional action in that direction.

With sincere gratitude,

Hope

Dear Hope,

You. Are. Awesome. Thank you for sharing your extraordinary family with me. People don't talk this way. We are a nation with an insatiable hunger for *the more* and *the new*. Those are the conversations around most dinner tables every evening. What we don't have—and want. Invariably, we end up losing ourselves in the *too much*.

What you have started to create in your own family is a new understanding of a critical dynamic: the less we have, the greater value each item comes to represent, subsequently increasing our gratitude for each thing. More importantly, we begin to appreciate and value *each other* even more. The fewer things we possess, and the more significant each thing—the more we value those we love. If life is about finding meaning, and becoming inspired to live with intention, compassion, generosity, and love—we fundamentally enhance our outlook and our potential to live fully when we feel unencumbered by excess. In a culture saturated with *want*—this may be one of the most elusive surprises of our time. Hats off to you and your family for choosing a more meaningful life. In knowing you are out there, I personally feel hope and endless abundance. Thank you.

Sincere gratitude,

Evan

Abundance is not something we acquire.
It is something we tune into.
– Wayne Dyer

Now It's Your Turn

Ask yourself the following questions:

1. Specifically, what do you possess that you are grateful for?

2. If you had to get on a ship for the rest of your life, which items could you reasonably leave behind?

3. With those items no longer in your possession, how might you maintain or increase your sense of gratitude?

4. If you had the opportunity to experiment with the idea that *less is more*, what tangible items are you willing to give up today in order to test the theory?

5. If the intentional absence of excess creates the tangible space for abundance, what are you inspired to do with your renewed sense of joy and gratitude?

Dear Evan,

I have reached the tipping point. I am convinced my family and I have been suckered into buying things that don't serve who we want to be and what we want to do. Most of it just feels like junk food, empty calories. Added up, it's a lot of fat and our little home's waistband is stretched beyond what it can contain. Where I continue to get stuck is the things that *seem* useful. For example, we have so many sets of art supplies, books, clothes, sports equipment, and kitchen stuff.

Those things have the potential to support who we want to be and what we want to do, but they take up so much space. How do I pare down the things we *could* use someday?

Hope

─────────────────

Dear Hope,

Your home should be an immediate source for the few things that inspire you and serve you every day (taking into account seasonal fluctuations). Decide who you want to be and what you want to do, and select your favorite things to serve that purpose. Things that are easily replaced will show up when you need them. For most people, it's not realistic to maintain a hardware store, craft shop, toy warehouse, kitchen supply store, and university library in your home. It's just too much, which is why we call the places where we buy things "stores." Thrift stores and consignment stores are great places to supplement your supplies when you need something inexpensively. Unless you have the space for it, storing anything and everything that may be useful "someday" is an impractical approach to effective functional storage systems at home. Figure out what you need, and subtract everything else. When you discover you need something you don't have, it will come to you.

Evan

─────────────────

*Minimalism is not a lack of something. It's simply
the perfect amount of something.*

– **Nicholas Burroughs**

The summer after graduate school, I sold my house at the University of Maine. I packed my dog, my kayak, my mountain bike, a pair of K2 Missiles mounted with three-pin telemark bindings, a tent, a sleeping bag, and a giant duffle stuffed with clothes and climbing gear. I took ten days crisscrossing the Canadian border on my way from New England to Bend, Oregon. Upon my arrival, I spent two nights at a local campground before signing a one-year lease on a tiny cottage outside of town. I was there a total of four days before receiving an invitation to interview for a teaching position in Aspen, Colorado. So I packed up and moved everything—again.

My first year out of college, I made $27,500 teaching Aspen seventh graders about literature, writing, anthropology, and world history. For housing, I secured a 250 square foot historic mining cabin without heat or running water for $50 (yes, fifty) dollars a month from a generous developer with a soft spot for local teachers. A throwback to Aspen's silver mining era, my hundred-year old cabin was unnervingly sandwiched between two contemporary houses in Aspen's prominent West End neighborhood—where the average home sold for $3.5 million. That was in 1999. Today, in its place, there stands a bizarre monstrosity of glass, concrete and dark composite paneling.

When I first moved to Aspen, I brought my best friend, Eliot, who was a colossal Great Pyrenees mountain dog who swiftly developed separation anxiety and howled like a fire engine whenever I left him alone. Due to Eliot's noisy proclivities, I was frequently evicted. This occurred with clockwork inevitability. In the six years I lived in Aspen, I actually relocated thirteen times. On my slim salary as a teacher, and then working in Aspen's prolific world of non-profits, all of my viable housing options were *unique*.

Consistent with my childhood, I was already adapted to moving. I became quite good at traveling light, packing up quickly, and setting up someplace new. I'm an undeniably nice guy, but my sound-sensitive Aspen neighbors hardly cared for my nervous pup's incessant yowling, so I honed my nomadic gypsy skills even further. And moved, again and again.

Over time, my biggest asset became crystal clear. Everything I owned either fit inside of or lashed on top of my trusty Subaru. I could pack, relocate, and refurbish virtually any space in a matter of hours—and I did exactly that, frequently. The life of a perpetually displaced professional was surprisingly joyful. Necessity truly is the mother of invention, and I became expert at ingenuity and resourcefulness. There was almost nothing I could not acquire if an item was not already close at hand. Due to a lack of storage space, I became equally adept at passing things along that no longer served my immediate needs.

What I call the "hot potato effect" became a lifestyle of uninterrupted balance. I mastered the art of moving things along and manifesting whatever things I needed, virtually out of thin air. I traded my excess items of value at consignment shops, and haunted thrift stores to keep my thumb on the pulse of year-round inventory. I traded with locals and shopped around, scrutinizing every purchase for maximum value. I saved my money for the essentials, and never wanted for much of anything.

Nestled amongst Aspen's ultra-affluent, I happily ambled from one oddly paltry apartment to the next. Mind you, I never lived in squalor. As a thoughtful bachelor, my living spaces were always tidy, clean, and artistically designed. With very little money and very little hope of striking it rich, I was nevertheless blissed right out of my mind. I thrived because I discovered freedom from excess. If something didn't fit in my next matchstick ramshackle, it was left behind. In that freedom, I found happiness outside of owning *things*. I found bliss in Rocky Mountain adventures, community activism, professional development, and meaningful relationships. Home is where your dog is. Who we love, what we do, how and why we live—these are the things that matter most. *Indeed, everything else is just stuff.*

My *success* is derived from a lifetime of lucky happenstance. Due to seemingly outlandish circumstances, from early childhood I was forced to pare down, travel light, and find meaningful rewards outside of material possession. A relatively humble Aspen inhabitant thriving in arguably one of the world's most expensive communities, I lived comfortably in every flat I called home—feeling unencumbered abundance in every peculiar space along the way. During my years living in Aspen, in spite of the staggering opulence all around me, I discovered that my possessions never defined me. The only items I could afford to accumulate had to satisfy the only two considerations I've ever had around my *things*. **For each item I acquired, a thing had to support 1) who I wanted to be and 2) what I wanted to achieve. If it didn't pass that test, I simply let it go.**

I affirm that clutter is relative and scalable. People with chronic disorganization, on the farthest end of the spectrum, are commonly known as *hoarders*, also referred to by the medical community as people with hoarding disorder. Often this condition of chronic disorganization is associated with a wide variety of compulsions that warrant mental health interventions. This is a topic for a different book altogether.

On the other end of the clutter spectrum, we have iconic Type A personalities with strict propensities for organization, as well as minimalists who have renounced all but the most essential of earthly possessions. The rest of us experience clutter and tidiness (or both!) to varying degrees, with perhaps only subtle impacts on our health, happiness, and overall well-being. In pursuit of our own unique optimal balance, I recommend that we seek to find a happy medium between blatant obsession, sheer complacency and utter hopelessness. Ask yourself who you want to *be*, and what you want to *do*. If a *thing* does not inspire or serve that purpose, it goes.

Today, working as an organizational solutions and strategies consultant, my work is focused on helping people to dig their way out of the mountains of dross that have absolutely consumed us. But here's the good news: we can reclaim our lives and fill them with intention and purpose. We no longer have to be defined by the meaningless shows we watch on television, or the crap we bring home from the mall. We can get rid of our junk. We can turn off our televisions. We can go outside. We can play with the dog and our children. We can stop looking for things to collect, and start thinking about what matters most to us and our families. If our things hold the greatest value, it may be time to rethink our lives—our very purpose for being.

Eaden and I pour our heart and soul into everything we do. When we need help, we only hire the very best. Upon completion of our new home, Intentional Solutions came highly recommended by our interior designer. Once we saw what Evan could do, it wasn't long before we invited him to work his magic at our business. Evan's mastery of organization and effective systems has transformed our operation. We're hooked. Evan is an absolute joy. – Deva Shantay

PART 2

LET'S GET
TO WORK

Going back to a simpler life is not a step backward.
– Yvon Chouinard

4

3 STEPS TO SUCCESS

Dear Evan,

Thank you. I've started this conversation with my family and everyone agrees we have too much stuff. I can feel myself shifting and the energy in our home has lifted to a level of optimism I can honestly say I didn't expect. My kids have been surprisingly enthusiastic, and my husband and I have started fantasizing about upgrades we'd like to make once we've cleared out and cleaned up. We've already begun sorting things to get rid of, but now the piles are everywhere. I'm afraid the kids will start shopping the piles, and we'll regress. We're so busy during the week, the process has stagnated a little. We've kind of gotten stuck with what to do next. We're ready for your super simple, ridiculously easy three-step method. Thanks!

Hope

Dear Hope,

Getting to acceptance and resolve is the hardest part, so congratulations! Once you've shifted your thinking and feel ready to roll up your sleeves, it's just a matter of plugging in my framework for action. This is the quick step-by-step summary. Make sure you do these steps *in order*, or you'll just be moving things around and getting frustrated and overwhelmed.

1. **SIMPLIFY** (Purge anything that isn't absolutely essential.)
   a. Trash
   b. Recycle/Upcycle
   c. Thrift/Gift
   d. Consign/Sell/Trade

2. **CLARIFY** (Organize everything that is absolutely essential.)
   a. Like Things Together
   b. Easy to Find
   c. Easy to Reach
   d. Out of the Way (Proximity = Urgency)

3. **INSPIRE** (Design your spaces with vibrancy and style.)
   a. Aesthetic
   b. Function
   c. Flexibility
   d. Lifestyle

REPEAT

Let's connect this week, and I'll talk you through it in more detail.

Evan

Frameworks are curricular tools designed to provide a platform for understanding, parameters for operation and conditions for repeatable outcomes. I hold a master's degree in experiential education and curriculum development. Having reliably utilized The Intentional Solutions 3-Step Method with countless individuals of all ages, from all walks of life, I present this framework with absolute confidence in its ability to deliver practical steps that build towards consistently desirable results.

Side note: I'm a big believer in don't change what you're doing, if it's working for you. I would not presume to direct someone away from blossoming in their own unique way. However, if you should attempt my system, these steps are highly recommended in the order prescribed.

The Intentional Solutions 3-Step Method has three core steps and four sub-steps for each step. (Get that?) Three steps. Four sub-steps. (3:4 might make it easier to remember.) **Before we get into the steps, we start with Stephen Covey's Highly Effective Habit #2: Start with the end in mind. In order to know what direction to go, it's always helpful to have an ideal vision of where we'd like to end up.** First, try to imagine the final product, the end result, the culminating outcome. In as much detail as possible, visualize what it will look like, feel like, sound like, even smell like. Create a multi-sensory map, if you will, to help define how we'll know when we've been successful. Once you have a mental picture (or an actual picture—Pinterest, catalogs, vision boards, and scrap books are great for generating ideas), it's time for step one.

What I'm about to share is extraordinary, life-changing, and so empowering that it could change your approach to everything you do. It's so *universal* that it applies to children, adolescents, adults, and seniors with equal accessibility and practicality, no matter who they are, what they do, or where they live. It's so *timeless* to the human condition that should people still be around two hundred years from now, they'll be able to use it effectively with the same reliable results. It is as *fundamental* as the gravity keeping us on the floor.

I'm talking, of course, about the Intentional Solutions 3-Step Method. Do anything better and live happier in three steps. Not four, seven, or twelve. Three. Use it to simplify, gain clarity, and achieve long-lasting inspiration with the stuff in your spaces—or leverage the formula for developing complex concepts and theoretical ideas into practical applications.

My work with clients targets five primary areas of life: organization, operational systems, time and task management, content creation, and professional networking. That's it, and if you think about it—it's everything we do. I would invite you to apply these three steps to anything that could benefit from a little simplicity, clarity, and inspiration. The process has been strategically designed to be easy to learn, easy to remember, and easy to apply. It's so easy, in fact, you'll be ready to get started almost as soon as it's explained—and you may already be doing it on your own before you finish this book!

How I help people answers: who we are, what we do, how and why we live. Getting off the track of sheer momentum and choosing a life of strategic intention changes the game. It starts with three simple steps. We start with the stuff in your space, because that's easy for people to understand right out of the box. Believe me when I say, your stuff, and *your space*, it's just a metaphor. Often, our spaces are representative of other areas of our lives, and making shifts in our physical space can enable so much else to transform. This process applies effectively to the tangible and intangible alike. So, here's my invitation to you. Try it.

Step 1: Simplify

Most people who attempt to get organized quit before they start because they become overwhelmed. When there is so much in front of us, it's difficult to see what we're looking at, much less know how to make any real headway. This is the "forest through the trees" effect. When it comes to the physical stuff in our spaces, step one is paramount. We must simplify first. Put another way, *we must purge that which is not essential.* To skip this step and move straight to organization is to inadvertently dig holes just to fill them up again. Unless we purge first, we're simply moving things around. When we purge, we sort items into four sub-categories:

- Trash
- Recycle and/or Upcycle
- Thrift or Gift
- Consign, Sell or Trade.

Step 2: Clarify

Once we have purged anything and everything that is not essential to 1) who we want to be and 2) what we want to achieve, *we must organize that which is essential to the life we seek.* Effective organization requires a means for rapid retrieval, convenient access, and ease of both functional and archival storage systems. The Intentional Solutions' Rules of Organization are broken down into four sub-categories:

- Like things together, so items are
- Easy to find
- Easy to reach, but
- Out of the way.

The formula "proximity = urgency" helps to determine how near or far an item should live based on how frequently or urgently it may be needed.

Step 3: Inspire

Everything good requires upkeep. Similar to fitness, good business, or running a high-performance automobile, general maintenance is required to maximize optimal performance. Inspiration provides the two essential ingredients for consistent and reliable performance, 1) ownership and 2) accountability. When we own something completely, we adopt it as an extension of ourselves and feel compelled to steward its inevitable success. Refreshing our spaces (interior design) is often the most fun, and therefore unfortunately, most people make the mistake of skipping the first two steps. This is a good way to spin our wheels, leading to designs that don't necessarily support ideal outcomes. When refreshing our spaces for "intentional interior design," we must first purge and organize before considering the next four sub-categories. Each space should be designed around the ideal:

- Aesthetic
- Function
- Flexibility, and
- Lifestyle.

That's it. That's the whole show. Three steps, executed in order—over and over again—in any space, under any conditions. 1) Simplify 2) Clarify 3) Inspire—Repeat.

Dear Evan,

We've hit a stumbling block. We've all lost a little momentum with our purge. The general feeling around the house is we're not really sure what to get rid of, what we can live without, what serves who we want to be and what we want to do—and what doesn't. We had buy-in that there's too much stuff, but when it comes to loading things up to go away, there's just not enough commitment for follow-through. It has also been busy and therefore harder to schedule the work. Both my husband and I came from families that tended to hoard every little thing, and we're seeing those genetic influences in ourselves—and in our children. Without someone standing over me telling me what to do, it's been difficult to motivate and follow the steps enough to see any kind of significant results. Honestly, I wonder if this is just how it is. Then I see how some people live *without* clutter, and I'm reminded of what I want. Help!

Hopeless

Dear Hopeless,

I hear you. It's true. This process is not easy. If it was, we wouldn't be talking—and I'd be out of a job! There is a cool concept I'd like for you to play with that might help you work through some of these challenges. I call it the Inspiration Triangle. Imagine three points of a triangle. The top point we'll call "inspiration." The bottom two points we'll call "ownership" and "accountability." The triangle cannot hold its shape without maintaining the strength and integrity of all three corners.

Think of it this way, when you are hungry, you *own* that hunger—it's undeniable and intrinsically motivating to take some action to alleviate the hungry feeling in your belly. You want to eat. That *want* provides enough accountability for you to engage in some intentional action. You become inspired to take action on behalf of what you want for yourself. You become an advocate for ensuring you get what you want, no matter what. Once you eat, you reinforce your appreciation of the benefits that come with nourishment. If you're smart, you create a lifestyle that supports eating on a regular basis, in order to maintain those benefits. It looks like this:

Ownership of Want + Accountability = Inspiration to Act.

There will always be obstacles to success. But when you finally commit, the rewards will be that much sweeter. You can do it. Let's talk this through and get you back on track. You can do this!

Evan

Never Mind. I Give Up.

I always preface my work with clients by stating, "I'm not going to tell you anything you don't already know." However, people often affirm that my distinctively simplified framework helps to inspire understanding and purposeful action. While most who attempt this work realize profound and long-lasting impacts, there are those who inevitably self-sabotage. Sometimes we subconsciously create "reasons" why things won't work and excuses not to follow through—and that becomes our reality.

Among those who express a desire for the benefits of this process, these are the most common obstacles to success that I've heard along with my responses to each of them.

"I'm just not an organized person. I come from a family of hoarders. I just can't do it."

• Nobody starts out a master. Like anything, to become skilled, we must practice. Most people just need opportunity, patience, and resolve.

• With a little structured support, we can leverage proven-effective strategies that help develop expertise over time.

"I can't do it without someone standing over me telling me what to do."

• Literally, this guide is written using the identical phrasing used during my detail-oriented, proven-effective one-on-one work with clients.

• Start with one small section at a time. Schedule blocks of time when you can focus, uninterrupted. Work that space from floor to ceiling, following my step-by-step instructions in order, you will discover that you can be an inspiring force in your own success—and the success of those around you.

"I can't do it. I just don't have enough time."

• This work can be time consuming, that is true. Although, clutter and time management challenges tend to perpetuate an endless cycle of hopelessness and complacency. The key is realistic block time, scheduled with the same importance as significant obligations.

• The truth is, when we live in a cluttered state of disorganization, we waste an inordinate amount of time looking for things and tidying up ineffectively. For those who think they don't have time—the result of this work literally *makes* time. Simplifying your life, getting organized and feeling inspired in your spaces will energize you to create time for the things that matter most. Stick with it and you will see for yourself.

Pull yourself together. Revisit your ideal vision and then recommit. You'll get there, one step at a time. Just keep going. You'll be so glad you did!

With four young kids, a ranch and a relentless schedule, Evan was just what I needed to feel like I was in control again. He helped me implement simple systems to manage my time, streamline my files, and organize my kids' spaces. Dialing in everything from our fridge and food pantry to my home office, and the mud room, Evan is a joy to work with and skilled in his methodology. I know we will be using him again. I could not recommend Intentional Solutions more highly.
– Rebecca Bier-Moebius

Simplicity is the key to brilliance.

– Bruce Lee

5

RECIPE FOR ORGANIZATIONAL BLISS

STEP 1: SIMPLIFY (PURGE)

Trash

Recycle & Upcycle

Thrift & Gift

Consign, Sell & Trade

PART I: WHY TO PURGE

Purge. The word all by itself just sounds horrible. In general, people cringe when it rudely intrudes itself in on the conversation. It conjures images and reflexes we tend to repress. What we forget, is that it is as natural as breathing. The simple act of breathing can alter our mood, our physiology, and our ability to regulate cognitive function. Do this exercise with me while you read the following:

We breathe fresh air into our lungs, which provides oxygen rich blood to our brain, which reminds our body to work. (Inhale deeply through your nose, hold it for a moment before exhaling completely through your mouth. Do this a few times now.) When we exhale, we let go of carbon dioxide toxins building up in our lungs. Fresh air goes in, toxic gas goes out. In…Out. We get what we need, and then we let go. In…Out. In…Out. In…Out. It feels wonderful, especially when we do it with thoughtful intention. (See "Notes on Meditation" later in this chapter.)

The same way that holding our breath can become poisonous to our bodies, holding on to *things* we no longer like, want, or need strangles our ability to regulate healthy lifestyles. Because we live in a consumer-centric culture, we tend to over-emphasize the *incoming* flow, rather than a more balanced approach to what comes *in* and what goes *out*. I get a lot of clients who ask me to organize their stuff. I'll be honest: for me, organizing is not the challenge. Sorting through relentless mounds for similar items, I could very easily organize forgotten puzzle pieces, barbequed fish skins, and poopy diapers into neatly labeled, designer fabric-covered bins, expertly arranged on shelves *just so*. Clearly, this would be a silly thing to do. And yet, the organizing industry has us buying containers of every shape, size, and finish, rather than encouraging us frenzied consumers to just *let things go*.

I won't pretend this comes easily. There are as many reasons why people hold on to *things* as there are things to *collect*. To the intellectual collector, their reasons seem perfectly sensible. But a lot of what we keep, we develop love-hate relationships with over time. The reminder of a lost loved one, the sadness of an unrealized future, the memory of a cherished time or relationship—these are powerful emotions that can become paralyzing. These feelings are tangible, valid, and profoundly influential in what we let go, and what we reluctantly embrace.

I usually ask clients to consider if the memories or feelings associated with a certain thing are being honored by the thing itself, and further, by the way a thing is kept. For example, a favorite Skype client based in Manhattan refused to give away a favorite t-shirt he never wore, because it was a gift from his father during a memorable trip to Prague. I suggested, perhaps the memory would be better honored by framing the shirt, and hanging it on his wall, rather than leaving it folded and forgotten at the bottom of his drawer. I was recently gifted my great, great aunt's crystal wine glasses, and rather than saving them for special occasions, we use them all the time. Every once in a while, one is accidentally broken—and it's a celebration of her life. Somewhere, I know she's happy I am using and enjoying her 150 year old crystal.

In organization, as in life, the parts that give us joy, support who we want to be and what we want to do are the only ones worth holding on to. For the rest of the things that come into our lives, it's really okay to use those things up and then let them go. With a little practice, we find that when we become clear on what we need most, those things *appear*. We may be surprised how refreshing life feels with a little less stuff and a little more breathing room.

Dear Evan,

We have made serious headway. We now have a designated laundry basket that circulates our home to help gather the things that no longer serve us. Every Friday, we deliver items to local thrift and consignment shops, per your recommendation. The kids have piles in their rooms of the clothes, books, and toys they're ready to part with and we've set up consignment accounts in each of their names to give them a little incentive to move things along. Our local consigner gives us added discounts if we use our accounts to trade up for items in the store, rather than cashing out. We're on the get-rid-of-2-or-3-things-for-every-1-new-thing program—and our lives are already starting to feel lighter. More importantly, we love our stuff! If we don't love something, it goes away and helps to fund things we do love. My husband and I help keep an eye on how much we are thrifting, so that a good portion of our stuff is donated philanthropically. Everything is starting to become automated, and we feel good about this direction.

However, I have been procrastinating on dealing with our family heirlooms. My husband and I inherited so much from both of our families, and there are things we DON'T love, but feel horribly guilty getting rid of outright, and nobody else in our family wants them. Help!

Hope

Dear Awesome,

Sounds like you have taken the bull by the horns and have regained some measure of control over the stuff in your life. Remember, the less you have, the easier it will be to manage. Therefore, the more space you will have to enjoy the things that matter most: who we love, what we do, how and why we live. You're on your way!

Guilt was the old you. The NEW you makes intentional choices on the basis of what serves who you want to be and what you want to do. Let's explore that further together ASAP.

Evan

GUILT

No amount of guilt can change the past, and no amount of worrying can change the future.
– Umar ibn Al-Khattab

Guilt, n.: *A universally treasured affliction dutifully carried with pride and self-righteous indignity.*

No matter your family's cultural heritage, religious practice, spiritual or ethnic roots, guilt is most likely woven into the threads of your subconscious like an awkward paper doily sewn into the seat of your underpants—just under the surface, and always a little irritating. It's there to remind us about serious matters, like obligation, allegiance and purpose. Guilt is there to keep us in check when we *ought* to, when all we want is *not* to.

I say, enough! Guilt can go and leave you to make decisions on your own. When working with my clients, I usually discover these feelings are predominantly associated with family heirlooms and gifts. Antique dining sets for 27, massive pieces of outlandish furniture, archaic pastry mixers, strange knitted garments, dreadfully over-styled artwork, aged greeting cards, sad wildlife-themed calendars, oddly sized collared dress shirts, and miscellaneous knick-knacks. In fact, I have seen maybe hundreds of thousands of relentless trinkets that seem to breed in the cover of darkness.

These are not items we like, nor want, and yet we reluctantly cling to them like live organs ripe for transplant. These items choke the viable spaces from our homes and burrow ever deeper into the recesses of our conscious. We feel shamelessly obligated, passive-aggressively cursing whatever unnamed umbilical cord that lingers between these objects and our loved ones and memories, year after guilt-loving year.

I tell you, there is no need. Let me explain. Items that are given as gifts are exactly that, gifted from someone else to you. If it is true that it is the thought that counts, then the intention of the gift was, in fact, the intention itself. As the recipient of that gift, it is your undeniable calling to acknowledge that thought and reciprocate with a dutiful and heartfelt gesture of your own. The original thought of generosity was acknowledged with a returned thought of gratitude, and the intention has come full circle. The actual gift—*the item*—has become irrelevant. It is the thought that counts. So, ditch it. Sell it. Upcycle or re-gift it. Burn it in a hole in the backyard or send it off down the river, but *let it go*.

It matters not how we come to acquire these undesirable things. The refreshing truth is we need not remain encumbered by them. We have an obligation to ourselves to take control of the stuff in our space, to gracefully deny the claws of guilt's timeless grip. It's time to turn a corner, leaving behind our old baggage. If you must, gently explain to your gifter that you have intentionally chosen to scale back, that you are consciously taking steps to simplify your life—even that you think enough of them and their gesture to include them in your process.

Do this preventatively with loved ones who are prolific gifters of *things*. (Grandparents, that's you!) Ask for their support, and be prepared to make a few suggestions. Or do what you must, quietly and behind the scenes. Most of your friends and family will support you—or never need be the wiser. Your heart will tell you what is right in any case.

You will find a peace in this process, an unexpected veneration to those you mean to honor. You will find that those still with us are surprisingly understanding, supportive—or perhaps indifferent. For those cherished souls no longer with us, well… most of them know your heart and love you just the same.

PART II: WHAT TO PURGE

The 80/20 Rule

When I am clutter-coaching with a client in their spaces, one of my first questions is, "How much of this can go away forever?" Often, my clients struggle with how to approach a specific answer to this seemingly overwhelming question. This is where I describe my version of the 80/20 Rule. Paraphrased, it goes something like this:

> *In general, most people truly only love about 20 percent of the stuff they possess. About 80 percent of their stuff, they do not love. Since we only love about 20 percent of our stuff, about 80 percent of our space is preoccupied storing everything else. Simplifying our stuff and refreshing our space is not as much about how we organize what we have, as much as it is about loving what we keep.*

The wonderful thing about the 80/20 Rule is that it can apply to almost anything. When you adopt this concept, you can improve your outlook and reprioritize any aspect of your life. Try exchanging the word "stuff" for whatever happens to be relevant for you right now. Think about your life: what people you hang out with, how you spend your time, what foods you eat, what television programs you watch, what music you listen to, what books you read, what thoughts occupy your conscious and subconscious mind. All of these concepts can conveniently be applied to the 80/20 Rule with equal scrutiny.

The primary question becomes who do we want to be and what do we want to achieve in this lifetime? Anything that does not directly support these two questions largely becomes irrelevant. A simple life is one unfettered by immaterial fripperies or extraneous encumbrances, and purely supports deliberately purposeful action. It is this elusive state of simplicity that often provides the necessary conditions for clarity of mind and inspiration of purpose. Those who find it become the role models we seek to emulate.

I work with a wide spectrum of people, including parents, students, teachers, retirees, CEO's, executive and program directors—many with exceptional success in life, some with considerable affluence, and others who can scarcely afford practical amenities. The one thing many of them have in common is the lack of an effective understanding of how much is enough, and how much is too much.

The point of the 80/20 Rule is to attempt to leverage what is available to us without constantly having to step over and work around things we don't like, want or need. Whether we are downsizing or creating cabinet space, closet space, living space, room to park the car in the garage, or brain space to think more clearly—purging that which we do not require fundamentally simplifies *who we are* and *what we are able to achieve*. While circumstances constantly shift, so does our focus, our priorities, and that which we need to be effective.

The easiest way to determine what to keep and what to toss has a lot to do with the practical consideration of how much room you have for functional and archival storage (a topic we'll explore in the next section). In short, decide how much space you are allocating for a particular kind of thing—whatever doesn't fit goes away. That means prioritizing each item to see what gets tossed, in order to make room for items that serve 1) who we want to be and 2) what we want to do.

With a little practice, this process becomes fun and habit-forming in a relatively short period of time. When we get good at it, everything we see brings us unquestionable joy. In effect, we flip the 80/20 Rule on its head, loving the vast majority of our intentional lives—and the *things* in it. More importantly, the results are virtually instantaneous. When a thing is physically removed, it leaves behind tangible space. When we utilize that newly available space with intention, life becomes infinitely more meaningful. And my experience is that most people hardly remember or care what was tossed, after it crosses the threshold.

Dear Evan,

We are back on board! I have officially enrolled my husband. He has become an enthusiastic, if not militant participant in this process. However, in cleaning out our home office and getting control of our household files, we could use a little guidance in managing our bills and other paper documents that continue to clutter the counter tops of our kitchen, dining table, office desk, living room corner, etc. How is it that we are still cutting trees down to support these obscene volumes of mail?!

Hope

Dear Hope,

My family and I have gone almost entirely paperless. With local office supply outlets and business centers, when we absolutely need to print, it's worth it to spend the dollar or two to get something on paper. Otherwise, everything is digitally reviewed, statements are emailed, bills are automated—and the sky hasn't fallen yet. It works for us and I recommend it, but it's not for everyone. That said, I have a simple process for managing all the paper in your life. Let's set up a little time to talk this week.

Evan

A Practical Word About Paper

We are horrified by our prolific mounds of household paperwork. They crush us by the weight of their awful importance. They are the utility bills, mortgage statements, bank summaries, investment portfolios, and income tax returns. They are our restaurant receipts, invoices, insurance claims, paystubs, medical bills, cellphone contracts, and financial loan statements. They are the endless lists scribbled on legal pads, sticky notes, and scratch sheets—accumulating for years, even decades. For better or worse, these are the official papers that give us validation and legitimate standing to the financial powers that be. They are the things we think are important, at least at any given time. Managing these documents effectively gives us the freedom to safely navigate unpredictable fiscal waters with relative agility.

There are a few guidelines, but unfortunately no one-size answer for every household or business. First, invest in a household shredder. Your personal information is the key to identity theft. Criminals sifting through the garbage have become inconceivably clever at ripping us off with our own trash. Don't believe me? Ask anyone whose life has been completely hijacked by information fraud. Shred every document you don't keep. You'll thank me the next time you hear about it on the news. Next, consider a scanner for electronic archiving. Folders neatly organized on your computer are manageable and easy to retrieve, but should always be backed up on a secure cloud-based server and/or an external hard drive.

I have reviewed several reputable sources to assemble consistencies in what most financial advisors and government agencies recommend. Disclaimer: I am not a certified public accountant, fiscal manager, or financial planner of any kind (thank goodness). Things change, so I strongly urge you to check with a qualified tax accountant, attorney and/or financial planning professional about your specific circumstances. At the time this book went to print, the following information was available online using a general keyword search "household documents to save and for how long":

- The IRS can audit you for no reason up to three years after you have filed your income tax return. If you omit 25% of your gross income, they can audit up to six years later. If you neglect to file altogether or file fraudulently, there is no statute of limitations on when they can show up with an audit. I have listed several items that can reasonably be destroyed after one month, one year, three years, and seven years. But the IRS isn't the only agency that may require documentation. For that reason, *the seven to ten year rule is the safest* for any record or document that may be tied to medical treatment, mortgages, income tax returns, litigation, or insurance claims. In general, for most people:

- Hold on to warranties until they expire or the items can no longer be returned or exchanged. For *one month*, maintain ATM printouts and bank statements until you can check them against your monthly statement for accuracy. If bank statements are your only means to prove a tax-related purchase, maintain for at least three years.

- For *one year*, maintain the following unless used for income tax purposes—then keep for three years after filing: paycheck stubs until you can compare to W2 and annual social security statement; utility bills; cancelled checks; credit card receipts; bank statements; and quarterly investment statements.

- For *three years*, keep the following: income tax returns; medical bills; and cancelled insurance policies. Maintain all records of selling property or stocks. Retain receipts, cancelled checks and other documents that support income or a deduction on your tax return. Any annual investment statements should be kept for three years after the investment is sold.

- Any records of satisfied loans and questionable income tax returns should be saved for *seven years*.

- For matters that are *still active*, maintain: contracts; insurance documents; stock certificates; property records; stock records; pensions and retirement plans; property tax records; disputed bills (until the dispute is resolved); and home improvement records (if indicating income or losses on tax return, save for three years). Investment records should be saved as long as you own the securities, plus seven years to prove capital gains and losses.

- Items to *keep forever* include: marriage licenses; birth certificates; adoption papers; death certificates; immunization records; college transcripts; current passports; and records of paid mortgages. These, along with current medical directives, wills, living wills, living trusts, and durable powers of attorney, should all be kept securely stored indefinitely in a fireproof/waterproof location or within a safety deposit box at the bank.

For more information, contact a reputable CPA or visit these useful online resources:

http://www.usa.gov/Topics/Money/Personal-Finance/Managing-Household-Records.shtml

http://www.oprah.com/money/Suze-Ormans-Spring-Cleaning-Overhaul-Your-Files-and-Finances_1/2

http://www.goodhousekeeping.com/home/cleaning-organizing/important-papers-to-keep

Part III: How To Purge

This is where the rubber meets the road. Roll up your sleeves, turn up the music and get ready to transform your space—and regain control of your life. These are the four sub-steps that spell out how to simplify the stuff in your space—*any* space. Again, I'll reaffirm that I'm not telling you anything you don't already know. However, it is my experience that following these steps in order improves our effectiveness by a factor of ten. You will need bins, boxes, tubs, or laundry baskets, each with a label corresponding to the four categories below.

- Trash
- Recycle & Upcycle
- Thrift & Gift
- Consign, Sell & Trade

I. TRASH

This ought to be pretty straight forward, but from my point

of view, it seems a little clarification is required. If it looks like trash, smells like trash, feels like trash, (do I have to?) *tastes* like trash—people, it's trash. *Throw it out.* If you don't know what it is, and the people closest to you can't identify it, pitch it. Most things in question are either obsolete or replaceable. With very few exceptions, things nobody can identify that haven't been used in years probably won't be missed. My general rule goes something like this: If a thing hasn't been used in god-knows-how-long, and is likely to be easily and/or affordably replaced, go ahead and pitch it, especially if it takes up a fair amount of real estate.

If you absolutely insist on keeping mystery items, decide up front how much space you'd like to allocate to these spare bits you find scattered about. Anything that doesn't reasonably fit, goes away forever. Trash can seem time consuming, but doing it first speeds up the process in the long run. Start with the floor and work your way up one corner of the room, maintaining constant movement and focused attention. Then move from one corner of the room to the next. Stay focused. All you're doing here is removing the trash. When your bin fills up, remove it, get a glass of water, and keep going.

Different Types of Trash

I spend a lot of time clearing out, cleaning up, getting organized, and beautifying spaces. Well-intentioned clients hoping not to be wasteful convince themselves that hoarding their old stuff is infinitely better than sending items to the dump.

We all do it. Unsure how to dispose of our treasured junk, we inevitably end up slaves to the stuff we care least about.

Not all dumps are created equal. Communities across the country are improving their local reclamation services intended to process a broader range of salvageable goods and materials. Specialty vendors also accept viable lumber, construction materials, paint, metal, auto parts, furniture, appliances, electronics, and other household items for resale. Often schools, community colleges, and local nonprofit organizations are interested in items that support programming, such as current sporting goods, audio-visual, computing, and photography equipment.

II. RECYCLE & UPCYCLE

Here's your chance to do your part for the planet. Reduce. Reuse. Recycle. Companies like Patagonia, Inc. have helped lead the global effort to re-use plastic bottles in polyester fabrics. Ingram Micro, the world's largest technology distributor with operations on six continents, along with UPS and EBay are launching some of the largest e-recycling efforts in history. Should not these practices become required for industrial production of all goods and materials? To me, it's just responsible business.

That's straightforward, and most communities are now set up to take the full spectrum of recyclable materials, but what about *up*cycling? If you are hip to the whole recycling movement, you may already know about the *über* design-savvy practice of converting *whatever* into something better. Virtually anything can be repurposed into something else, but upcycling implies a design-element with astounding practicality and extraordinary style.

The practice, of course, is nothing new. The indigenous people of the world have been effectively multi-purposing every scrap and bone for tens of thousands of years. With the surge in global manufacturing over the last fifty years, however, today's consumers have grown accustomed to satisfying every conceivable (and inconceivable) need with a fresh-from-the-factory, plastic-wrapped piece of merchandise, painstakingly processed, shipped and sold at full retail prices in a local big-box discount store near you. Effective, community-supported upcycling efforts may be the future to locally sustainable economies.

I believe there is already enough, in terms of goods and materials, out there that we can probably slow down production for a little while. With so much of our household and industrial junk ending up in landfills and ocean-floating waste dumps, it's naive to believe we actually need more *stuff* to be made from scratch at the factory level. Upcycling on a large scale, however, is gaining momentum.

Upcycling on a grassroots level is just as important and arguably more interesting. As consumers increasingly look for cost-cutting designer alternatives, nothing beats local artisans for creative craftsmanship and originality. Anyone can piece a few bits and pieces together, but it takes the truly unique to transform the mundane into the elegantly divine. We are seeing this across the country. People are carving out financially viable niches in commerce, using second-hand resources available to them locally. This may be the dawn of the rebirth of the re-purposefully re-creative. (Say that five times real fast.) Upcycling promotes local consumerism, barter-based economies and self-reliance—at a time when every exit off the interstate looks identical to the one before it, with the same big-box shopping centers and the same plastic-wrapped merchandise packed in packaging enough to circle the globe a dozen times. Why not promote a little creative use of the stuff already in hand? Why not insist on it?

With times as tight as they are, with so much hanging in the balance, with so many struggling to maintain basic existence, why not tilt the odds in favor of sustainability, humility, and re-purposefulness? We have proven our capacity to do so much with the finite resources available to us on this planet. As we continue to witness the impacts of our hubris on the climate and failing economies across the globe, perhaps now is the time to reconsider our relationship to the stuff in our lives. Perhaps now is the time to reconsider what we *require*, and what else may satisfy the need. Perhaps now is the time to make more effort to ensure the items we discard have the opportunity to serve another purpose. Perhaps now is the time to recommit to taking some personal responsibility for what we purchase, where those things comes from, how they were manufactured, and if our intentionally re-creative touch helps to make our stuff infinitely more meaningful.

For inspiring ideas and more information on practical upcycling, visit: www.UpcycleMagazine.com or two other great websites: www.UpcycleThat.com and www.HipCycle.com.

III. THRIFT & GIFT

There is a thriving industry dedicated to the de-construction of commercial and residential structures, specifically targeting the re-use of viable materials for second-hand construction. Habitat for Humanity retail ReStore outlets are commonly the recipients of such materials, although there are increasingly for-profit firms focused on this niche. For property owners looking to tear down and rebuild, donating professionally de-constructed building materials to Habitat for Humanity can provide significant tax deductible incentives for donors.

While re-use and recycling operations help to redistribute potentially viable materials for resale, many items contain harmful substances that necessitate regulated disposal. Paint, fluorescents, batteries, petroleum products, toxic compounds found in a variety of household and industrial chemicals, as well as appliances, should absolutely be directed to the proper facilities most suited for responsible disposal. Efforts to improve recycling operations now include elaborate electronics, computer, and cell phone deconstruction centers designed to maximize reprocessing potential for items previously regarded as landfill waste. Your local dump should be able to recommend the suitable facilities for the items you seek to dispose of. The goal is to return as much viable material back to production and to keep as much toxic material out of the ecosystem as possible.

Proprietors of consignment and thrift stores are happy to discuss the items they are most inclined to take and when. As seasons change, local stores tend to shift their respective inventories to reflect the demand for what is likely to be most lucrative in the coming months. So, don't be offended if there's no interest in your old board shorts in December, just label your bags and bins out of the way until the following season.

Thrift stores are not nearly as picky as consignors, but tend to fill up at peak seasons and turn donors away. If your stuff is stained, torn, shredded, broken, or trashed—it's probably garbage, but check with your local soup kitchen, clothes drive, or place of worship. Thrift stores are inundated with items that nobody wants to buy. Please be considerate about your items' condition, current potential value, and subsequent resell potential before dumping at local thrift stores. Despite your good intentions, they usually don't want your old, worn-out, outdated, damaged junk. Not sure? Call ahead.

Getting in the habit of purging your belongings several times a year helps to keep this on-going process relatively simple. Keep bins labeled for each season to maintain a year-round system for moving things out. Keep a dedicated laundry basket in your home that travels throughout the week; fill it with items you want to get rid of. At the end of the week, deliver the items in the basket to their respective outgoing locations. **Most importantly, reducing what we accumulate in the first place has the biggest cumulative impact overall. It's the best way to ensure our stuff doesn't end up owning us.**

IV. CONSIGN, SELL & TRADE

Consignment retailers only want the finest, like-new or immaculately conditioned items in their community. Some shops specialize in certain things and get pretty strict about their inventory. Shop owners need to maximize every square inch of their showroom floor. That means scrutinizing every item for its income potential. If you are trying to consign your stuff, call ahead or browse to learn who moves which items at the highest prices. There are local shops who specialize in furniture, antiques, rugs, jewelry, clothes, kids' stuff, sporting goods, and so on.

If you've got stuff to sell, learn which stores are consistently moving inventory and make friends with the staff. I pay for the gas in my car with the cumulative income from my accounts at local consignment stores. I've coached low-income clients on how to stock up on affordably priced high-end merchandise from thrift stores, and make money by flipping them at higher end consignment boutiques. This type of commerce recycling moves inventory and encourages sustainable demand among a variety of shops, which helps to stimulate local economies. Meanwhile, people learn to become second-hand savvy.

EBay and other online outlets are great for specialty items where local interest is low. Estate sales are most lucrative with strategic marketing and premier merchandise. Garage sales are usually a waste of time. Unless you want to perfect effective online or garage sale tactics, leave it to the pros who are set up to move merchandise efficiently with the best chance for getting a reasonable return on your behalf. Craigslist and the local classifieds are the best exception: anything posted at low or no cost to a wide buying audience minimizes risk, time commitment, and hassle. Just watch for scams—cash, PayPal, or verified checks reduce your risk of falling prey to fraudulent buyers fishing for naïve sellers.

There used to be a time when local economies were based solely on the barter system; a carton of eggs for a bundle of wool, some milled lumber for a dairy cow, a lesson in this for a hand with that. Cooperation and shared resources for the collective gain held the highest value, the greatest good. A return to this model may help restore some measure of balance for individuals and communities struggling to make ends meet.

I'm no economist, but I've personally experienced the benefits from voluntarily trading goods and services. I've seen it effectively supplement tangible income when cash was not readily available. A willingness among neighbors to cooperate, share, and pull the collective weight helps create thoughtfully intentional communities that thrive. When we strategically integrate the barter system into local economies, we provide incentive for everyone to contribute. By leveling the community playing field in this way, individuals are more inclined to take responsibility for themselves and also develop something of value for others.

Trends indicate that entrepreneurialism is on the rise. Whether out of sheer desperation or creative will, more people are successfully launching their own wares and services. In a wide array of industries, local entrepreneurs are carving viable economic niches where none existed before. When we combine the spirit of the barter system with the ingenuity and innovation of small business, we empower up-and-coming entrepreneurs to flourish.

In 2012, when I decided to create my consulting firm, I had no idea what to do or how to start, so I reached out to individuals in my community who had experience with small business. My network turned out to be extensive. There was expertise in business creation, management, finance, marketing, strategic planning, program development, branding, and more. I was saved by a community of individuals willing to share what they knew, many times in exchange for whatever I was willing to trade in return. Over time, their collective knowledge became integrated with my own practice. A viable business was thereby created from a little self-determination and the generosity of others.

In an effort to share the practical methods of my own success, I created Bonedale Business Cooperative, a hyper-local Facebook group of entrepreneurs in my own community who are willing to share what they know. Our informal organization is really just a loose-knit crowd of small business-es and nonprofit leaders eager to support one another. There's no membership fee, just a simple understanding that every-one is invited to contribute something, someday. The more participation, the stronger the group, and the more beneficial membership becomes to everyone involved. Participation is encouraged to be informal—over coffee, in living rooms—or over a pint at our local micro-breweries.

Members are encouraged to host a workshop, teach a class, write a testimonial, share a product, donate some time or ma-terials, network a little, collaborate a lot, and help each other grow. Peppered throughout public venues around my com-munity, the Bonedale Business Cooperative is designed to be casual, impromptu, and responsive to the needs of its mem-bers. Without any cumbersome bylaws, membership fees, or governing executive committees, we are simply a group of people informally reaching out in support of one another.

If you are a fan of strategic trade, consider what you need and start shopping around for it. Spread the word that you are willing to offer a trade for items you seek, and keep a run-ning inventory of skills and assets available to you that may be appealing to prospective traders. When considering trad-ing items in exchange for your services, just be mindful of the value of the item(s) you are trading for. Do not inadvertently undervalue your precious time.

Dear Evan,

Your claim is that your three-step method is universal in its application. I'm wondering if you can help organize thoughts, ideas—thinking itself. My oldest has a lot on her plate managing the pressures of her school studies, athletics, extracurricular activities, standardized testing, and her responsibilities at home. She's fried, and it's starting to wear on her. Upset, she told me the other day she "needed Evan to organize [her] brain." How does your method apply?

Hope

Dear Hope,

It's true. Clutter is a metaphor. Mental clutter is real; it's not just a figurative thing. And the impacts of mental clutter can bog us down in the same way as the physical messes in our space. When we feel overwhelmed with the details of our lives, we will experience long-lasting benefits by applying the 80/20 Rule to our thoughts. Simply, we must purge from our brains all that we can in the form of day planners, project management tools (I recommend Trello.com), and other ways to organize that information externally. This frees our minds to focus on one thing at a time. Meditation helps, as does consistent downloads that help capture and process data—one topic at a time. Let's set up a time to talk about this more with you and your daughter at your earliest convenience.

Evan

The 80/20 Rule of Your Brain: The Mental Purge

From time to time, I work with clients who say they can't think straight, and they often ask if I can help clear their mental clutter. I'm no intellectual gymnast, but there is a concept I frequently use to help people develop some measure of cerebral clarity. Taken from the 80/20 Rule, the word *stuff* can be taken in the literal sense, or as a metaphor for other *things*, in this case, thoughts in the mind.

When it comes to cognitive clarity, the 80/20 Rule works wonders for your brain. Most of us walk around with any number of unruly bits of information cluttering up our mind. Some items are neatly organized and properly stored for convenient retrieval. Fortunately for most of us, the important stuff is autonomic (breathing, digestion, moving around, homeostasis, etc.). Then there are items that are pretty handy for instant recall, like our name and how to put pants on. Add a shopping list and key details from a conversation with your boss, and it's no wonder we forget where we're going and the names of our children.

Dumping the minutiae out of our brain and into strategic systems (for example time and task management, project management) designed for effective storage and rapid retrieval helps disentangle the thinking part of our brain for, well, *thinking*. Creative problem solving and attention to detail dramatically improve with two things: practice, and clutter-free capacity for thought. Start accumulating too much clutter, and we clog our brain's ability to effectively focus and process what is right in front of us. Even really smart people need to get creative about data retention in order to keep sharp.

There is no truly effective multi-tasking, there is only doing multiple things simultaneously with marginal to mediocre results. We live in an age constantly bombarding us with useless distraction. Turning those distractions off and downloading some of that content out of our brain gives us the mental bandwidth to help focus, stay present, and think clearly. Meditation is far and away the oldest and one of the most effective forms of purging our minds, bringing renewed focus, clarity and perspective.

MEDITATION: PURGING THE MIND FOR MENTAL CLARITY

Until recently, I've never been one for meditation. The formality of it seemed a little too—ceremonial. A meditative *practice* always seemed like, well, a lot of fancy sitting. I mean, seriously. Sitting still, eyes closed with excessive posture and thoughtful breathing, weird incense stinking up the house, not thinking about anything in particular...it just seemed like a big waste of time. Well, it turns out I'm an idiot. Add this to the colossal list of things I got *wrong*.

I recently realized that I need meditation. I need the intentional breathing. I need the mind-dump. I need the break in the action. I need the quiet. I need those few moments away from my work. I need the peace away from my spirited daughter, and the minutiae my wife and I seem to hash out with tireless enthusiasm. More than anything, I need the space away from myself. I need the chasm of calm and silence away from my relentless monkey mind. I need to know I can go there in an instant, so far from the noise and the chatter. Amidst the chaos and exhilaration of my life, I need to know that place of stillness lives within me, and that it's mine to access whenever I want it.

I practice a Vietnamese style of martial arts called Cuong Nhu. There are two schools in Colorado's Roaring Fork Valley where I train, both with highly accomplished instructors and a national reputation for depth and substance. At the start and finish of each class, there is a moment of pause for meditation. The time is set aside for intentionally grounding in this moment, leaving behind emotion and distraction in order to become fully present in the now, fully accepting of new teachings, fully aware of a higher potential for growth free from all judgment. In the conclusion of those brief moments, I increasingly realized that I craved more time. I wasn't ready to come back. I needed more time.

I now experiment with a meditative practice of my own. I look for a moment of quiet and I sit up straight, cross-legged on the floor, hands resting on my knees. I close my eyes and I allow my mind to drift. I pay no attention to anything in particular, and observe fleeting thoughts float by like clouds on a summer day. In those first few moments of stillness, I do something I never do. I. Let. Go. I give up. I experience my being without judgment or preference. It is as though the top of my head opens up and I slip away, connecting to the far away vastness of dark serenity. I don't know where I go, but coming back is one of the most re-invigorating experiences I have come to know.

I must have been living under a rock. I am amazed to discover how many people I know swear by their meditative practice. In addition to our flexible yogis and hippy existentialists, it turns out there are distinguished CEO's, corporate moguls, executive directors, and powerfully influential entrepreneurs and community leaders around the planet who adhere to their own ardent practice as a part of waking up and doing business. The result is a powerfully restorative effect on one's ability to show up with clarity and resolve.

Knowing who we are and what we are meant to do in this world can be a daunting struggle between grief and hope, failure and triumph. Nothing is certain, just as nothing remains constant. In the midst of so much turmoil, confusion, doubt, and sadness in the world, anything that can restore the inner light is worthy of a little time and cultivation. Anything we can do as individuals to purge our minds, rekindle our inner flame for courage and love, to remember our shared cosmic roots, to reconnect with the collective consciousness; these small things have a tangible impact on how we show up for ourselves and each other on the planet. I think that is worth a few moments of fancy sitting.

Like snakes shedding their skin to reveal rejuvenated, healthier surfaces beneath, we have explored the necessity and benefits of simplifying first. The next chapter will focus on achieving clarity through a structured process of organization.

Step 2: Clarify (Organize)

Like Things Together

Easy to Find

Easy to Reach

Out of the Way (Proximity = Urgency)

Organization is the Zen of putting things away utilizing systems designed for rapid retrieval, convenient use, and effective storage. Using the Intentional Solutions Rules of Organization, you can master organization of literally anything in four simple steps. Before we get into the steps, let's briefly discuss the important distinction between tools and systems. Tools are the variety of implements we use to physically manipulate our stuff. Systems define the process by which things are manipulated. These steps describe one system using two tools (labels and containers).

The Intentional Solutions
4 Rules Of Organization

I. LIKE THINGS TOGETHER

This is not a unique concept, but rarely is it implemented well.

The premise is simple: all the parts and pieces of a thing are stored together for rapid retrieval, convenient use, and effective storage. Pasta with pasta. Socks with socks. Screw drivers with screw drivers. Gloves with gloves. Tennis balls with tennis balls. Bean soup with bean soup. Band aids with band aids. When I need to find something, I know those things live together. Obviously, this concept is scalable, but simple.

II. EASY TO FIND

This is the "find" factor. Items need to be located as needed, and not a moment sooner. This requires storage. I recommend logical labels and/or transparent containers for items that are put away.

Labels help achieve consistency and household (or community) buy-in. Many of my clients insist on fancy label-makers, but I find them to be expensive and over-rated. Blank labels (of which there are an infinite variety), computer-generated stickers, and neat hand-written labels all work equally well. Labels should make sense to all users in order to ensure understanding. Expect to dial down your labeling a couple times in order to reduce ambiguity and redundancies. Families that struggle maintaining organizational systems usually lack clear labels for what goes where. Once things are labeled, everyone knows the intended system. If labels are disregarded, the conversation turns to *why*. This becomes an opportunity to respectfully engage with those unable or unwilling to participate. (Explore my *Negotiations* process on the blog page of my website to learn more about effective compromise and conflict resolution. A simple keyword search will pull it right up.)

Containers should appropriately fit the shape, size, and volume of the objects inside. I recommend transparent containers with lids. I'm not picky about brands, but sturdy products will deliver the most return on your investment. I much prefer to store food items in glass if I'm able to. Sturdy see-through plastic bins work well for items stored on shelves, or when stacking is unavoidable. Bins (of infinite variety) should be utilized with function in sync with aesthetic. I can't tell you how many times I've worked with designers who purchase expensive, stylish bins with little regard to the contents of what will go inside them. Design your shelving and bin storage purchases around what needs to be stored—not the other way around.

I use the term "container" to indicate an expandable concept for any vessel that effectively holds "like things together." Open shelves, racks, drawers, cabinets, dressers, lockers— entire rooms, even buildings can effectively contain our stuff. As an example, think of a garage as a container for your automobiles. Containers should be scalable, with the ability to collapse and expand to support sub-sets of the same "like things." As an example, think of a filing cabinet holding paperwork, subdivided into appropriate categories for the variety of files therein. The system for this tool can be applied to your food pantry for bins containing different types of pasta or snacks, as well as for art supplies with separate bins subdividing items used for different types of crafts.

III. EASY TO REACH

This is the "convenience" factor. Items should be readily available and within convenient reach when needed. Where we store items should correspond with the intended user(s) in mind. In fact, I specifically design systems around the user(s) most likely to *struggle* putting things away. I want things to be so easy that there are no excuses not to put things back where they belong. That means storing items and containers in places that are easily accessible for others.

Because I am tall, strong, and motivated, I am much more willing to work a bit harder to put things up and away. A little thoughtful consideration helps encourage household buy-in, so I reserve the prime real estate for those I hope to enroll in my systems. For example, we have eight bikes in our garage, neatly organized on a variety of racks and ceiling hooks. My wife's bikes are on the lowest, easiest to reach rack, so she will be more inclined to put them away when she's done riding. It's worth it to me to maintain a clutter-free garage and put my bikes on the ceiling hooks, rather than ask my wife to strain herself trying.

My daughter's toy bins are neatly lined up on her floor, easily accessible when it's time to put everything away. (Anything still left on the floor at bedtime, she knows I'll give away! Yikes! Learn more about www.LoveandLogic.com parenting.)

IV. OUT OF THE WAY

This is the "clutter" factor or "sprawl effect." So, if we're going for "easy to reach, but out of the way," how do we know where to put anything? Simple. **Proximity equals urgency.** The more urgently we are likely to need something, the more convenient it should be to retrieve. That way we're not frantically on a search and rescue mission for the car keys when it's time to hit the road. The items in your life that command the most attention ought to live in convenient locations for their imminent use. The Halloween decorations should be stored in a labeled bin in the garage until next year. If your Halloween stuff is cluttering up your living spaces in April, my guess is these items are taking up valuable real estate worthy of your consideration. Think about your refrigerator. The stuff you reach for all the time ought to be front and center. That Korean paste you use a couple times a year should not be in the way of reaching for fresh produce. Proximity equals urgency.

MAXIMIZE VERTICAL STORAGE POTENTIAL

Clutter tends to breed on horizontal surfaces. When I assess spaces for optimal organization, I'm usually looking for ways to maximize vertical storage potential. This helps to leverage viable living spaces by reducing the storage footprint. The less amount of space in the room allocated for storage, the more space for me to live my life unencumbered.

FUNCTIONAL STORAGE VS. ARCHIVAL STORAGE

Broken down simply, there are two storage categories: 1) things we use all the time and 2) things we hardly ever use. Functional storage serves the things we utilize often enough to warrant prime real estate for imminent use. Archival storage items include income tax statements from two years ago and the seasonal items not needed for another six months. This is a "proximity equals urgency" thing, so carefully scrutinize your spaces and systems accordingly.

MORE ON STORAGE

Storage is a specific concept with an ambiguous definition. Simply, it's a means to hold something for future use. Without further description, that's pretty vague. And when I work with my clients around their personal and professional storage systems, it shows. Clarifying what is worth storing and *how* has an important impact on understanding why we hold onto things in the first place.

People tend to dump and cram items "for future use" anywhere they can—without very much intention. If they can drop it easily or cram it to fit, that's where it goes. Efficient retrieval of those items becomes about as impractical as maintaining any kind of useful inventory. When things accumulate over time, we tend to pile our stuff out of sight. That gets costly.

According to the Self-Storage Association, the United States storage industry generated more than $24 billion in annual revenues in 2014 alone. Widely regarded as the fastest growing segment of the commercial real estate industry over the last 40 years, Wall Street analysts consider the industry to be recession resistant. This begs the question, what's in all those big metal containers? I bet I could tell you what's in a lot of them, and it ain't pretty.

The good news is that systems for storing treasures for future use are exactly the same, no matter if we're talking about love letters, grandpa's golf clubs, or electronic files on your computer. Whether comic books, baseball cards and stamp collections, antique furniture, vintage automobiles, or family heirlooms, *how* we maintain those items is just as important as *why*. It starts with getting some clarity on what is important to you.

When people feel guilty about holding on to something they don't want, use, like, or need, that's usually a pretty good sign something is ready to be passed along. I always suggest upcycling, recycling, thrifting, trading, and consigning items that may still hold value to others. Those are viable alternatives to the dumpster, or worse—paying to store junk indefinitely in a storage unit until we're dead.

In my practice, I help clients identify storage-worthy items and create systems around two different types of storage: functional and archival. That distinction alone helps to provide clarity around which systems and what tools are most effective. *My* freakish brain looks at everything in one of two ways: something is either a container or something to go *inside* a container. With the Russian doll effect, good containers nest easily inside other containers, creating expandable systems that are as efficient as they are effective.

A filing cabinet is a good example of the "Russian doll" effect. Documents that may need to be retrieved for future reference are organized into similarly categorized file folders, grouped together in hanging folders, sorted by topic into similar sections, drawers, and filing cabinets. Every element of the system is logically labeled to reflect its contents, nested together, and strategically positioned in order of priority based on urgency. This system is universal and scalable and applies to anything, including physical objects, digital files, and intangible ideas.

For functional and archival storage systems, items utilized most frequently are grouped together in the most convenient locations. Items used less frequently, are stored in progressively less convenient locations. I refer to this as primary, secondary, and tertiary storage, and it applies to anything we may want to save out of the way for future use.

Using Intentional Solutions' 4 Rules of Organization, sort items storage-worthy in the following ways: 1) like things together, so that they are 2) easy to find, 3) easy to reach, but 4) out of the way. But before you do, make sure to purge everything that does not directly support 1) who you want to be and 2) what you want to do. Clean out, get organized, and spend more time enjoying the people you love and the experiences that make you truly happy.

ORGANIZATION IN ACTION

Dear Evan,

Our home is looking its best since we moved in over ten years ago! So much so that we decided to throw a party. Our kids spent the night at friends' houses and we had about twenty couples join us for dinner and dessert—something we haven't done in years! Thank you! Our friends and neighbors took a tour of our home all "cleaned up" and organized, and I can tell you, *you* have become a pretty popular guy among our circle of friends! Everyone was sharing stories about where they need you in their lives—and in the lives of their families. Here's a great example:

My next door neighbor and his wife own an SUV, a pickup truck, and a small RV. Like us, they have kids, hobbies, and a ton of stuff! James was asking if you could help him clean out his garage, so he could park not one—but both cars indoors before winter comes. I reassured him, if anyone could help—it was *you*!

Hope

Dear Hope (& James),

Congratulations on hosting what I'm sure was a beautiful evening in your gorgeously rejuvenated home. It's that kind of feedback that gives us the motivation to stay inspired to do the maintenance to keep it going month after month, year after year. When the culture of your place shifts, your lifestyle shifts to support 1) who you want to be and 2) what you want to do. Like runners training for marathons, it gets easier.

James, I live in the high Rocky Mountains of Colorado, so I also value parking my cars indoors during our snowy winter months. The steps are simple. Simplify, as in purge everything that is not absolutely essential to 1) who you want to be and 2) what you want to do; Clarify, as in organize your stuff 1) like things together, so things are 2) easy to find, 3) easy to reach, but 4) out of the way; Inspire, as in design your space so you are able to aesthetically, functionally, and flexibly utilize the garage to suit your lifestyle. Pulling your shiny ride into an immaculate garage is one of the nicest conveniences I know. And once you've got your systems dialed, you'll never go back! Let's connect soon.

Evan

THE GARAGE

In the midst of Rocky Mountain winters, a garaged car owner is blissful, relaxed, and more likely to start (and finish) each day with a gleaming smile. As winter descends and dark, frigid mornings dig in for the long, cold season, there is something deviously luxurious about pulling the daily commuter into a clean and spaciously well-organized garage. Actually, the luxury comes in the morning. While the neighbors are frantically stomping around in snow boots, desperately coaxing their frozen vehicles back to life, my wife and I listen to their furious ice scraping with triumphant satisfaction. Burrowing deeper into our cozy bedding for an extra twenty minutes, we gloat with delight knowing our hibernating Subaru is smugly resting in the warmth of our immaculate garage.

While the notion of parking an entire automobile in the garage is mere fantasy for defeatists, optimist go-getters decide it's their inalienable right to clear their garage-clutter once and for all, and permanently carve out an unobstructed piece of hallowed real estate for the venerated family wagon. Truth be told, it's not that difficult to accomplish—and may be one of the single most rewarding achievements of the whole year. Sure, it may seem daunting, considering the current state of your garage, but undertaken with tactical precision and focused intention, you'll have Ol' Bessie (or in our case, Aunt Sally) sitting high and dry in no time.

Let's review Intentional Solutions' 3-Step Method. 1) Simplify, 2) Clarify, and 3) Inspire. In other words, purge what you don't need, organize what is essential to keep, and refresh the space to inspire long-term success. Schedule some time on a Saturday afternoon when you can devote three to five hours of uninterrupted time. Going through the entire space, account for absolutely every single item, starting on one side of the garage, working from floor to ceiling. Each item represents a potential obstacle to parking, so scrutinize every article with unwavering conviction. *Purge, purge, purge.* Whatever can be gotten rid of, the larger and more effective the aisle around your potentially-parked vehicle for viable use of car doors. After all, parking the thing without use of the doors may result in equally frustrating challenges.

Sorting what you keep using Intentional Interiors' 4 Rules of Organization, 1) like things together, 2) easy to find, 3) easy to reach, but 4) out of the way, will ensure that everything from ski equipment to toilet paper is easy to find, easy to reach, and out of the way. Refreshing the space for aesthetic, function, flexibility, and your personal lifestyle should effectively inspire enough family support and personal commitment to maintain your palatial new indoor parking—though you may inadvertently annoy the hell out of your frigid, sleep deprived neighbors.

There are all manner of contraptions and apparatuses to aid in your garage organization, ranging from pulleys and straps to hooks, elaborate shelves, and cabinet systems, but avoid spending a dime until all that can be purged is sufficiently removed from your space. Re-use, repurpose, and upcycle anything that may be useful in storing items effectively—even if it's not as pretty as the catalog picture. You can always spend your disposable income on designer storage bins later, if you simply cannot live without them. The best use of a functional storage space incorporates vertically-designed systems. Using floor-to-ceiling shelving, compartments, cabinets and so forth helps to ensure optimal vertical square footage while helping to minimize horizontal sprawl. Bins should be labeled, seasonal summer items should be secured out of the way, and consideration to safe passage throughout your space should be paramount.

I've worked with countless clients to design simple, elegant, and aesthetically functional and archival storage spaces—but none quite as rewarding as preparing a household garage for winter parking.

Dear Evan,

My best friend had a few girlfriends over this weekend for a little girl-talk over wine and cheese. *Your* name keeps coming up! My friend, Lauren, was saying how frustrated she gets preparing meals for her family. A working mom and community volunteer, she just doesn't have systems in place to plan for meals. Inevitably, she ends up with fast food takeout or buying items at the store she already has, while things end up going bad in her fridge because she doesn't know what's there. Her house is beautiful, and she's organized in every room—except her fridge and pantry. How can we use your systems to help her? Thanks.

Hope

Dear Hope (& Lauren),

I've learned that clutter comes in all shapes and sizes, and when we look closely, we've all got a little clutter-hound deep down inside. One of the biggest household expenses comes with providing nourishing meals for our families. Creating systems to keep us organized in the kitchen will create more time for preparing deliciously inspired, well-balanced meals—as well as saving money on items we really don't need. Let's schedule some time to talk kitchen systems—it's easier than you think, and will inspire a better culinary experience for the entire family.

Evan

THE REFRIGERATOR

When it comes to your family's bottom line, I usually head for the kitchen. When you can see your food inventory at a glance, you'll save money at the market. Creating a few simple systems in your kitchen will help save time and money and help create practical spaces for functional storage and food prep. Like everything else, I recommend the Intentional Solutions' 3-Step Method: 1) Simplify, 2) Clarify, and 3) Inspire. With only a few hours of focused intention, your kitchen will become a staging ground for creating nutritious and appetizing meals, as well as leveraging your household budget.

Most of my clients are usually mortified by their refrigerators, so I usually insist we begin there. Clear the counters and the kitchen table to create a little room to work. Next, completely empty the contents of your fridge. Everything comes out. As you handle each item, sort everything onto the counters. Anything that is trash or recyclable goes right into the appropriate bin. Everything else, I recommend my 4 Rules of Organization: (1) like things together, so items are (2) easy to find, (3) easy to reach, but (4) out of the way. For now, we'll put condiments with condiments, meats with meats, produce with produce, etc. Once the fridge is entirely empty, we'll wipe it down with antibacterial cleaner. Getting in there seasonally helps to keep your fridge from really getting funky. (Believe me, I've seen it all!) After everything is wiped down and really shiny, start putting things away.

By now, you should have already purged the old stuff and the mysteries. If you're not sure, it's not worth the risk, so toss it. Check to make sure you don't want to adjust the built-in shelves to accommodate taller items (beverages) or shorter items (eggs). I suggest putting things back using my formula "proximity equals urgency." To review, the more frequently you need to get something, the easier it is to reach. In our fridge, the top shelf is for stacked, see-through leftover containers, so we can easily see what needs to be eaten first. The shelf below is split for eggs, meats, and cheeses. The next lower shelf is medium height for bowls of fresh fruit and vegetables, which need to be easily seen and readily eaten. The bottom shelf is for tall beverages, stacked yogurt containers, and other big stuff that needs some height. The top drawer is fresh produce for the week. The bottom drawer is just for baking, everything labeled in Ziploc® storage bags. The door shelves includes a rack for vitamins, peanut butter and jellies, condiments, homemade salad dressings, marinades, chocolate, and the yummy stuff my wife uses to make Indian and Thai food. Use dry-erase markers to label containers and lazy susans for convenient access to every corner of your fridge. I like mason jars and glass Tupperware, but re-purposed strawberry and spinach containers are also effective for putting like things together in containers. Repeat this process with your freezer and food pantry.

Label your shelves, jars, bins, and drawers to help the family keep everything organized. You will be amazed how far you can stretch your grocery budget, just by seeing your food inventory at a glance. Keep a Ziploc® bag of coupons in your car. Pre-plan your meals in advance to know what you'll need for the week. Shop with a well-planned list. Never shop hungry. Prepare meals with flexible leftover options. Shop the outer aisles of the market. Try to eat real, minimally or non-processed foods with a variety of naturally-occurring colors, textures, and shapes. Keep your grains whole and your fruits, vegetables, and proteins organic. For everything else, only buy things you can pronounce. Read the ingredients. If there are more than a handful of ingredients, or you can't pronounce most of them, skip it. A sustainable budget is about leveraging available resources, so rip out your grass and grow a vegetable garden. Participate in a CSA (community service agriculture) or local permaculture program—or start your own. Local, organic food production will be the future of sustainable communities. (But that's a topic for another book.)

Dear Evan,

My brother-in-law and his family are avid campers. They stayed with us recently for spring break, and he commented on how well organized we have become. Dean was lamenting that he'd like better systems for their frequent camping trips into the mountains outside of Ashville, North Carolina. Surely, you have systems for getting organized with camping equipment. Ideas?

Hope

Dear Hope (& Dean),

Living in the Colorado Rockies, we're also outdoor enthusiasts and spend a lot of our summer months backpacking, car camping, and bikepacking. We have found that the trick to a smooth trip is to simplify systems and pack only the bare essentials that support 1) who we want to be and 2) what we want to do—*on that trip*. The key is only bringing the things you absolutely love and choosing strategic containers that work for your trip and means of travel. Let's talk ASAP and I'll explain.

Evan

THE GREAT OUTDOORS

My daughter was only three months old on her second real camping trip. My parents drove up from Phoenix for my first Father's Day weekend, and met us in the Lincoln Creek campground eleven miles outside of Aspen, Colorado. My dad and I went paragliding off Aspen Mountain; our women nervously watched us soar overhead and greeted us in a grassy field off North Star Preserve like soldiers home from war. That weekend we brought mountain bikes, climbing gear, a small raft, coolers, a guitar, and so much baby stuff—I still don't know how we fit into our creek-side camp site, much less our little Subaru. It's not always pretty, and there are no points for style, but we mountain folk love to get right up close and personal with nature.

Whether pitching tents, or sleeping out under the stars, there's no better way to enjoy the great outdoors than taking a good, old-fashioned family camping trip. Once spring has sprung, the bears return to town, and wildfire season is officially upon us, grabbing the kids and heading for the hills is what summertime in the Rockies is all about. Of course there are starkly conflicting breeds of outdoor enthusiast—from competitive rack-clad mountaineers to bivy sack soloists; from Pata-Gucci gear snobs to all-American Coleman-Cabela's camper aficionados. No matter your destination or the labels on your stuff, getting where you are going with ease and some manner of organizational prowess is likely to keep you coming back all season long.

Whether you are backpacking, car camping, or hauling multiple recreational vehicles in tow, you'll benefit from a little organization before you hit the road. Camping is all about two concepts I use with clients all the time: *contained clutter and functional storage.* The Intentional Solutions' 4 Rules of Organization work gloriously for any way you roll. You'll want to keep like things together (E.g., first aid kit, kitchen, pantry, gear, clothes, etc.), in separate labeled containers that are easy to find (Ziploc® freezer bags, plastic bins, or stuff sacks), so that containers are easy to reach, but out of the way. The containers you are most likely to use a lot (or in an emergency) should be the easiest to grab; less urgent items should be further away. In other words, in grizzly country, don't hide your pepper spray at the bottom of your pack!

Once in the car, tempting as it may be to load your gear on top of the kids, your journey will be more comfortable and safer if you can separate passengers from cargo. Soft stuff sacks, securely stowed, should be the only items packed with kiddos. Plastic bins should be transparent, clearly labeled, long and shallow with tight fitting lids. This enables you to find most of their contents at a glance without resorting to digging for hidden necessities. Stuff sacks should be small to medium sized, color-coded, or tagged with some kind of label for easy identification (E.g., the emergency first aid kit is the only bright red stuff sack in our gear). According to Moab four-wheeling standards, anything securely fastened to the exterior of your vehicle is fair game.

Once at camp, everything stays inside its respective bag, bin, sack, or bucket until ready to be used—and then promptly returned afterward. I've seen some wild looking campgrounds that are hazardous, dysfunctional, and organizational disasters when it comes time for daily basics like food preparation, kitchen management, relaxed lounging, and restful sleeping. Tidy campsites are safer, less likely to attract local wildlife (and would-be looters), and make enjoying the outdoors infinitely more comfortable for everyone. After your sojourn, returning your gear to pre-trip conditions guarantees that everything will be clean, re-stocked, organized, and ready for your next family adventure. As we mountain folk say in winter, "See you on the hill!"

Dear Evan,

My nephew, Jacob, is finishing his 9th grade year and struggling with high school. He's a great kid and a go-getter, but the last time we spoke, he was clearly frustrated by pervasive disorganization and the resulting academic challenges as a student. I was hoping you could give us some recommendations that might support him—as well as a few tips my kids could benefit from learning early. Thanks.

Hope

Dear Hope (& Jacob),

My first job out of graduate school was teaching 7th grade social studies and language arts at Aspen Middle School in Aspen, Colorado. From an educator's perspective, one of my greatest assets was remembering how disorganized I was as a student. Because I didn't see a lot of instruction on organization elsewhere, as a teacher, I made sure to integrate simple strategies into my curricula. Developing these skills early has a profoundly beneficial impact on the rest of life. Learning effective organizational techniques helps to develop executive function proficiency, giving us a significant advantage over our peers who may struggle with their studies, relationships, time management, and ultimately vying for rewarding positions in the competitive job market. Let's talk about specifically where Jacob is struggling, and I can share a few suggestions that may help.

Evan

STUDENTS

When I was a kid, going back to school was like getting gut-kicked into ice water. The transition from summer to the classroom was a disaster. Antics for missing the school bus were strategic, and executed with imposing precision. Shenanigans designed to confuse and enrage first-year, substitute, and re-tire-ready teachers were honed from an early age, effectively securing a permanent seat for me in the study-free confines of the Principal's office. During autumns of my youth, there was no limit to the obscure illnesses and stress-induced infirmities to keep me safely at home, away from a gauntlet of problems waiting for me at school. It is appropriately ironic that I would go on to receive a Master's degree in education and become a school teacher myself.

Looking back on my youth, it's easy to see why I resisted. I struggled with reading, writing, and arithmetic. I had difficulty concentrating and was easily distracted. I was ruthlessly bullied by older kids. I had no organizational sense for academics whatsoever. For nine months out of the year, my chaos festered. Despite emotionally and academically supportive, well-intentioned parents, I had no strategies, no coping skills, and no incentive for catching up. I clearly lacked the natural abilities of my classmates. I felt hopelessly behind. While the pretty girls with perfect braids and pristine penmanship pulled tidy notebooks from their immaculate book bags, I sat distraught with incomplete homework, a disheveled, below-average mess, eager to be sent out of the room.

I'm here to tell you, redemption is a wonderful thing. With a little direction, I got over myself and rediscovered initiative, determination, and talent. At some point, I looked up, and I was okay. Like most of us, students thrive when tools, spaces, and systems for learning are void of clutter, confusion, and distraction. As we experience incremental tastes of success, we cultivate a sense of ability, pride, and independence. With every success, we nurture our confidence and develop greater enthusiasm for life-long learning.

I have worked with students of all ages around organizational solutions to maximize clarity, confidence, and self-efficacy in and out of the classroom. There are a few tools and a few specific systems I recommend for everyone across the board:

1. A day planner is like a map of time. It shows the topography of what is ahead and helps plot a course of action for successfully reaching immediate goals. (More on this in the section about time and task management.)

2. A lot has moved to digital content, but for students who still use paper, three ring binders, spiral notebooks, and file folders help organize studies into categories and subcategories. When I was a kid, these materials and subsequent assignments were reduced to shreds in a crumpled mess at the bottom of my book bag before Thanksgiving break. Boys, especially, wear these things out quickly, so keep them replaced with durable back-ups throughout the school year. When one dies, it's a good time to review its contents, label it, file it for convenient reference, and start fresh with a sturdy replacement for the next lesson.

3. Maintain an organized workspace where students can spread out and focus on lessons without distractions. These clutter-free spaces, ideally, should be stocked with easily accessible materials required for typical

assignments, including the full assortment of office supplies and electronic accoutrements.

Going back to school can be fun for students who maintain control of the minutia required for organized learning. A few simple strategies go a long way when it comes to inspiring success for the long-term.

EXECUTIVE FUNCTION

The human brain is an absolute marvel of evolution. Our brains have the ability to manage a relentless onslaught of information, integrate new data with learned material, and coordinate sensation, subconscious thought, and focused problem-solving with instantaneous and complex movement—all while maintaining auto-regulated homeostasis. All of this happens in an instant, all the time, which is—utterly astounding. Considering everything that could go wrong, it's a wonder that things actually work as often as they do. In my business, I am fascinated by one particular aspect of human neuroscience, known as executive function.

Located on the anterior surface of the frontal lobe is the most recently evolved region of the human brain, called the prefrontal cortex. Frequently described as the air traffic control tower of the central nervous system, the prefrontal cortex is the CEO of human thought, directing all cognitive analysis and decision-making systems, referred to as executive function. Included in executive functions are judgment, prediction, expectation, determination, and regulation. Executive function isolates an individual's ability to effectively integrate concentration, working memory, cognitive flexibility, and inhibitory control. The complexity inherent in such multifaceted function helps to illuminate personality, emotional perceptivity, intellectual athleticism, and human sentience. It's not surprising that research now indicates that executive functions have a greater impact than IQ on an individual's overall success in life.

We know that the average human prefrontal cortex is not fully developed until the mid-twenties, which explains why children and adolescents often exhibit behavior lacking judgment and self-regulation. Students often struggle in traditional academic settings where executive functions are an assumed expectation. Young people especially, are often labeled and stigmatized rather than presented with supplemental assistance to develop executive functions. It is also proven that psychotropic chemical substances, trauma, and medically acquired brain injuries, such as stroke and disease can have profound impact on executive function. While a healthy, fully developed brain may improve cognitive proficiency over time, both adolescents and adults significantly benefit from strategic techniques designed to increase executive function abilities.

I often start with the question, 'Where do you feel stuck?' and then apply the three-step method from there. Step 1, Simplify: What is not essential that can be purged? This critical step helps remove the obstacles to success. Thinning the excess helps to see the forest through the trees. Step 2, Clarify: What is absolutely essential that can be organized? This sets the stage for establishing systems that promote ease of use and sustainable success. Step 3, Inspire: How can we bring this to life with style and vibrancy so that we are inspired to do the necessary maintenance for lasting results? This stirring process fuels self-determination and solidifies personal and collective resolve.

Executive functions have recently become targeted as an important component within K-12th grade settings, among higher education learners and through professional development opportunities in the work place. With a little structure, executive function can become second-nature, offering individuals a chance at a simplified, more rewarding, and more meaningful life.

TIME & TASK MANAGEMENT

I'm self-employed with no employees. I do my own marketing, promotions, programming, networking, business development, and work with multiple clients on a daily basis. I have a feisty wife who enjoys my company, and a precocious kiddo who keeps me on my toes. I make time to exercise, get out and enjoy nature, cook good food, goof off with friends, and sleep at least six to eight hours most nights. Our lives are full-time jobs. How to keep track of it all without losing our minds is key. I simply could not do it without my day planner. How or why people try is beyond me.

Time management starts with creating an intention. Decide how you want to spend your time, schedule your priorities, and commit to doing what you say you will do. That's integrity. Tracking your intentions in a day planner commits you to the priorities you have identified for yourself. Whether work, exercise, volunteer, or fun—when it's recorded in a day planner, somehow the universe clears the way for your success. **Leave it to chance, and there's no limit to what we will never do**.

I increasingly work with clients around time management, both personal and professional. Virtually all of those with chronic challenges either don't have a day planner or don't use one well. So, let's talk about tools and systems. The calendar industry is huge, bigger than huge, *absurdly* huge. Choosing a calendar is like choosing an over-the-counter allergy medication or granola bars. Half the time, people give up, close their eyes and hope for the best. Throw in nine and a half billion options for personal hand-held electronic devices, and it's enough to make people give up all together. They've got apps forecasting everything from menstrual cycles and caloric intake to e-calendars that chart everything from sexual performance to toddler potty schedules. It's turned into staying on top of everything—all the time.

So, let's simplify. The planner I use and recommend offers the traditional or academic year format. Both feature weekly *and* monthly at-a-glance calendars at full-size (8.5"x11"), and it is spiral bound with a flexible plastic cover (www.BlueSky. com). Blue Sky also makes three smaller sizes, all of which are useless—unless you have nothing to do. The full-size is about half an inch thick and works nicely on its own or fits into the sleeve of any leather bound folder cover. Every reputable office supply store carries them. Every June, I buy a new one and get comfortable breaking it in. On July first, I'm good to go with the new one and file the old for future reference. Yes, I understand the rationale for syncing cellphones with electronic apps and online systems. But when things go awry (fussy cell towers, power outages, cellphone submersions, solar flares, and zombie apocalypse), for me, nothing beats pencil and paper.

Let's talk systems. Every day, I schedule appointments into my monthly at-a-glance calendar with a pencil. Every Sunday night, I fill in the following week's appointments along with my prioritized to-do list into the week-at-a-glance. My wife and I sit down every Sunday night for about seven minutes to review the week, discuss logistics, and schedule our coveted date night. I call that the "Sunday sync." While there are minor tweaks periodically throughout the week, it's an effective touch point for us, promotes good communication, and keeps our expectations realistic. I have exceptional relationships with my family because "getting on the same page" is as easy as reviewing our planners and scheduling the fun stuff around our priorities.

My system works equally well for people who prefer digital platforms, or must straddle digital with a paper hardcopy. For online project management, I recommend the Sunrise Calendar app in sync with Trello.com. Time management doesn't have to be some nebulous mystery. Choose a planner. Use it every day. Talk to the people in your life. Schedule your priorities and then commit. Don't be afraid to ask for help. You'll save time, make time, and improve your time with the little time you've got left.

Dear Evan,

My aging father has increasingly struggled with dementia for the last several years. Our family has recently come together to talk about how to support him—and one another, through this painfully frustrating time. Borderline hoarders, my parents have amassed a lifetime of *things*. Their home is over fifty years old and in disrepair. The accumulation of their stuff has made caring for my dad progressively more difficult for my step-mom. As we pull together to clean up, clear out, organize, and make sense of their possessions, we're looking for systems to help streamline our effort. Eventually, we'll have you come out and give us a hand on-site. You mentioned that you frequently get referrals from hospice agencies and hospitals working with patients at the end of life, and I know you assist families with household items after people have passed. The family has agreed that we'd like to recruit you for your services to help us through this tough transition, as we prepare for the end. Sadly,

Hope

Dear Hope,

I'm so sorry. I've worked with countless families through this transition, including my own, and I know how emotionally demanding this process can be on everyone. I find that the key to getting through it is to go slow, take your time, get a little assistance where you need it just to take off a little pressure—and try to use the clearing as an opportunity to reconnect with the people in your family. I've seen families reconnect, share powerfully inspiring stories, make amends, and pass along the significant details of their lives through the process of going through a lifetime of possessions. It's a sacred time of clearing, reminiscing, and reprioritizing what life has meant—what lessons have been learned, and how we choose to understand the concept of legacy. I would be honored to assist you and your family through this important transition. Let's talk at your discretion to discuss scheduling and logistics. Warmly,

Evan

END OF LIFE

"I can't die yet—my house is a mess!" I hear it all the time. A lifetime of accumulated documents, furniture, photographs, clothes, and keepsakes can be overwhelming to deal with. However, making this a family priority can ease tension, soothe anxiety, and collectively unite families around individuals approaching end of life. The truth is our stuff gets exponentially more difficult to manage the older we get. The energy it takes to purge, sort, and organize can be exhausting, but for our elderly seniors the task often becomes impossible without help. When family members (often with the assistance of a professional) rally to help with this task, I've seen strained relationships healed, forgotten stories brought to light, and peace restored to individuals hoping to reconcile a distant past with an unfamiliar future.

Anyone with experience can tell you, after loved ones pass, the stuff that gets left behind doesn't get any easier to deal with. On the contrary, when we have the opportunity to learn first-hand what things have personal meaning, we gain the knowledge of perspective and can feel good about making informed decisions. We learn what is treasured, and what is just *stuff*. This cathartic process validates a lifetime of experiences and provides a productive setting for people to reflect, share, clean up, heal, and move on.

Far too often, our elderly seniors inhabit cluttered spaces, wrought with obstacles, hazards, and unwanted junk. The added value of taking on this project early is that de-cluttered living spaces promote calming and comfortable places to rest. Restful spaces are proven to reduce stress, improve healing, and increase overall health and happiness. This is why hospitals, hospice programs, rehabilitation facilities, and nursing homes are pouring hundreds of millions of dollars into interior designs that help to create tranquil recovery spaces. People approaching end of life are far more likely to thrive in spaces without clutter, where critical items are organized and easy to find, where the décor is thoughtfully designed to nourish the soul and help an aged heart to smile.

To get started, pick the room with the most significant *negative* impact. For an elderly senior, this could be a disorganized kitchen, a cluttered bathroom, or untidy bedroom. I encourage clients to work from the floor to ceiling. Examine every item, piece by piece and decide whether it is essential or can go away forever. Most seniors require assistance, though if piles are sorted into small, manageable sizes, often a lot of the work can be done without help. The key is to purge first and organize second. Explain that this work is essential for their safety and well-being.

Organize essential items (1) like things together, (2) easy to find in transparent containers and/or with clear labels, (3) easy to reach in convenient locations, and (4) out of the way to prevent dangerous hazards and sprawling clutter. Any items not enjoyed lately or after several seasons can probably go to local thrift or consignment stores. Files and documents should be clearly labeled in file boxes or cabinets, purged of outdated materials. With assistance from friends and family, clearly label photographs and keepsakes to help accurately record important details and treasured memories. There are a wide variety of services set up to turn old photos into quality books and digitally archived memorabilia. Video interviews are often an easy way to digitally compile relevant details about the family and an individual's life.

This process can be a beautiful, treasured experience with lasting and profoundly positive impacts. The key is to allocate time, get assistance where you need it, and keep an open mind and an open heart. It may be the most valuable thing you ever do for yourself and the family.

Dear Evan,

Increasingly, we have enjoyed hosting our friends and family at our home. We recently hosted an annual Home Owners Association dinner, and the topic of climate change came up. Watching the undeniable shifts in extreme weather patterns has us thinking about how we (as a family and a community) can take proactive steps. Between droughts, floods, blizzards, cold snaps, hurricanes, and heat waves—there are any number of meteorological (as well as human) scenarios that could necessitate some measure of self-reliance. As a strategies consultant, have you done any work helping people to organize their homes and/or neighborhoods in this regard?

Hope

Dear Hope,

I believe we have a moral responsibility to take proactive steps on our own behalf to ensure a buffer of safety and sustainability, in the event of an emergency situation. That means, reasonable food and water stores for everyone in your household for no less than two weeks. Getting organized as a household and as a community provides an added cushion of well-being, when everyone else is running around in a panic. With a little thoughtful planning, you and your community can create a model of self-reliance if ever circumstances turned ugly. Thanks for asking—this one is an important topic that I'm delighted to discuss with you and your HOA.

Evan

GET ORGANIZED FOR THE WORST-CASE SCENARIO

In the movies and in life, you know this to be true: Shit happens and people usually figure out how to accept, adapt, cope, or overcome. The world over, every generation has thought the sky was falling at one time or another. The modern carte du jour of viable ever-impending apocalyptic cataclysms is a tribute to our obsessive zest for ruin. Solar flares, asteroids, ubiquitous terrorist attacks, homicidal gunmen, climate change, civil unrest, disease pandemics, weapons of mass destruction, political upheaval, economic and societal collapse, alien invasion, flesh-eating zombies, and ingenious mashups of these are all very popular right now among Hollywood executives and survivalists digging fortified bunkers and stockpiling heavy artillery.

Whether or not you buy into doomsday conjecture, when it comes to responding to earth-shatteringly calamitous events, some small degree of common sense, basic preparedness, and community organization are great ways to stack the odds in our collective favor.

After doing a little research, I recently purchased a few books written by credible and widely acclaimed authors, whose levelheaded and unemotional calculations seem reasonably plausible. They deliver practical strategies for the average family, using stuff widely available, in response to just about any scenario—excluding *Sharknado, War of the Worlds,* and *Night of the Living Dead.* Whatever momentarily inconvenient hiccup to the system or unprecedented end-of-the-world game-changer, this I know for certain: my family and I will always need 1) potable water, 2) readily available nutritious food, and 3) a warm, safe place to figure things out.

FEMA now recommends that all families in the United States be prepared with a 72 hour "bug out bag" for unforeseen evacuations as well as a two-week emergency supply of food and clean drinking water. In the event of a local, regional, or global event, those who disregard such fundamental acts of practicality will likely be the ones wildly flailing about. In contrast, suppose you and your neighborhood had already made basic preparations; imagine if your entire community was organized—at least for an immediate emergency response—how much safer families would feel, relative to the communities who had done *nothing.* The more we prepare with basic necessities, the greater and more effective our cooperative buffer between calm and panic, rational response, and hysterical frenzy.

I'm not suggesting a specific course of action, per se. I'm simply inviting individuals to consider the discussion, and encourage families to do what feels most comfortable to them. I am a sensible pragmatist who sees the wisdom in learning the basics and taking reasonable steps to ensure my family and I have life-sustaining essentials, just in case (fill in the blank). Safety starts with clean drinking water and a few practical resources, including an organized community of people in support of each other. Knowing your neighbors, talking with loved ones about a plan, and learning the basics of what to do and how to do it provides a significant head-start if the lights go out and the tap stops flowing. With some thoughtful consideration, getting your household and your neighborhood proactively organized can be simple, affordable, fun, and empowering.

So, what if nothing ever happens? People make misinformed investments all the time, with tangible losses. In this case, if the zombies never come, if nothing descends upon us, if the most foolish investment I ever make is a little proactive planning to ensure my family and my beloved community are prepared for the worst—well, that's an investment I can live with. Literally.

Recommended Resources:

When All Hell Breaks Loose: Stuff You Need to Survive When Disaster Strikes. Cody Lundin. Copyright © 2007 Gibbs Smith Publisher.

The Doom and Bloom Survival Medicine Handbook: Keep Your Loved Ones Healthy in Every Disaster, from Wildfires to Complete Societal Collapse. Joseph Alton, M.D. and Amy Alton, A.R.N.P. Copyright © 2012 Doom and Bloom™, LLC.

Step 3 Inspire (Design)

Aesthetic

Function

Flexibility

Lifestyle

Congratulations! Step three is the most fun! If you've made it this far, you are ready to do a deep dive into realizing your ideal spaces. Drawing on elements of intentional interior design, strategic function, practical flexibility, and personal preference, we discover inspiration through ownership and accountability. In the spaces we create, we become motivated to do the maintenance required for long-term results. Sometimes a change of scenery is all we need to improve our entire outlook on life.

Design doesn't have to be expensive. In fact, I have personally designed innumerable spaces without spending a dime.

Clearing the cluttered path to the life we seek can be as simple as reconfiguring the things we love. I have found that when spaces stagnate over time, they can lose their potential to inspire. As a kid, I was known to rearrange the furniture in my bedroom several times a year—often in comical configurations that made absolutely no sense. Whether practical or absurd, my early proclivity for interior design always provided a unique perspective and a fresh approach to blooming wherever I happened to be planted. These days, helping clients to design clutter-free, well-organized, blissfully stimulating spaces is my passion.

Rearranging our stuff can effectively and affordably re-engage the senses and ignite the imagination. Well-configured spaces have the power to inspire productivity, purpose, serenity, healing, creativity, love, and harmony. Intentionally readjusting the things in our space may be the easiest way to give a fresh start to the life we seek and improve the relationships with those we love most. I applaud those who rearrange their stuff at least once a year to help rejuvenate the vibrancy of their home or business. I always encourage clients to make this process as simple as possible. Start with a few considerations for what I call "intentional interior design." When evaluating any space, ask yourself:

1. What is my ideal vision?

2. How would I like to feel in this space?

3. What do I intend to do in this space?

4. What other potential uses am I likely to require from this space?

5. What are my known personal preferences that may lend to designing a unique space that suits me?

Giving this process some thoughtful consideration helps to ensure an outcome that resembles the ideal vision, rather than arbitrarily laying things out and hoping for the best.

Your ideal vision is a good starting point to identify what we are working towards. Often, this is a mixture of sensations or images. Other times, the ideal draws tangible connections to specific genres, activities, cherished objects, or locations in nature. The more we can flush out what you see in your mind's eye, the easier to reproduce that vision. Often clients confess that they are not exactly sure what they are working towards, but they know for certain that what they've got just is not working for them anymore. Sometimes all it takes is objectivity and a little creative encouragement to affordably bring renewed aesthetic, function, and flexibility to the spaces of your home or business.

How we want to feel *emotionally* helps to shape our palette of color, texture, shape, light, sound, life, and finish in each space. For example, in our home offices, we want to feel productive and energized. In our bedrooms, we want to feel overcome by a restful sensation of love and tranquility. In our living rooms, we want to playfully indulge in complete harmony with friends and family. In our kitchens, we want to move with ease and purpose, inspired to create culinary marvels that healthfully nourish body and soul. Our exterior spaces stimulate a heartwarming connection with the natural world around us. If the rooms in your home do not support how you want to feel, it may be time to re-evaluate and get intentional about the layout and design of your space.

I. AESTHETIC

We should adore the spaces we inhabit. They should be expressions of our creativity, extensions of our soul and conduits for inspiration. The following are fundamental components of interior design to consider when transforming your ideal vision into practical reality:

- **Mood** is produced using the effective juxtaposition and fusion of furniture, fixture, finish, light, color, sound, texture, pattern, focal points, and theme. These elements help create a desired *feeling*.

- **Balance** is created by maintaining proportional *weight* in the elements configured in all quadrants of a space.

- **Scale** is an important principle that provides *uniformity* in a particular space, with an emphasis on dimension, proportion, and scope.

- **Flow** determines a space's ability to promote harmonious *movement*, including both traffic patterns and the circular flow of energy.

- **Genre** is defined by a specific style a space takes on, created by the combined effect of the full spectrum of elements used.

I recommend catalogs, architectural and interior design magazines and online resources to help my clients determine the styles that resonate most. My favorite online resource is www. Houzz.com, which boasts a prolific database of searchable images, also available as a mobile app. I particularly emphasize how clients can integrate new ideas with existing assets, to help reduce the costs (and clutter) associated with replacing things unnecessarily. In this way, we are able to prioritize the budget to maximize the result. Repurposing and refinishing existing pieces helps stretch a budget considerably. Paint may be one of the single most affordably effective ways to give a space a makeover. There are countless do-it-yourself resources to help generate ideas that reflect your ideal vision.

II. FUNCTION

Spaces must work. While we compile preferred interior design elements, we must ensure that they complement the intended use(s) of our spaces—for all intended users. First ask yourself what you intend to *do*. Spaces intended for eating, sleeping, working, playing, exercising, bathing, socializing, creating, and rejuvenating are all enhanced when we consider how each user intends to interact with the space during those activities. In this way, form truly follows function.

III. FLEXIBILITY

While some households have the luxury of a dedicated space for every specific activity imaginable, most of us require built-in flexibility to utilize our spaces in multiple ways. The classic example is the home office that doubles as a guest room; the media room that doubles as a home gym. Considering the limitations of your spaces, imagine how else you may intend to use each space, and structure your design to accommodate a wide variety of possible alternate uses.

IV. LIFESTYLE

Lifestyle encompasses how we interact with our space. I have a client who designed a climbing wall in their living room that wraps around three walls, sprawling twenty feet to a vaulted ceiling. I have another client who installed a dancing pole on a small platform stage in their media room. I have clients who have dog and cat doors installed in multiple areas to control the traffic of their pets. I have a client who has an interior slide running from an upstairs bedroom into the downstairs playroom. I have a client who has a fireman's pole from the master suite into the garage. I have clients with dedicated studios for work, art, music, meditation, exercise, and entertaining guests. While these design elements may seem eccentric (and expensive), they are scalable and represent just a few examples of how we can create spaces that personalize and invigorate what makes us passionate people.

When we focus on amassing *things*, arbitrarily arranging them in our spaces, we inadvertently forget what makes us human *beings*. Being: living intentionally through exploration and adventure, serving others, creating something new, growing as individuals, and collectively contributing to the common good. This is what it means to be human. Our stuff and space should only support who we want to be and what we want to achieve. When we shift our emphasis away from *thoughtless accumulation and decorating,* to creating spaces that *inspire an intentional life*, we exemplify the concept of "intentional interior design," and we thrive. Repeat these three steps over and over again, in every room of your home, in every corner of your business, in every stoop, hallway, and nook. Three steps. Over and over again. Simplify. Clarify. Inspire.

Dear Evan,

I wanted to write to say thank you. Thank you for helping us simplify, get some much needed clarity, and stay inspired to take actions that support who we want to be and what we want to do in this lifetime. Since working with you, my family has cleared out, cleaned up, organized, and even remodeled several rooms of our home. I now have a home office where I am currently working to start my own art distribution firm. My kids have permanently uncluttered bedrooms with intentional locations for quiet, focused study—and all seem to be thriving in school, at home, and in life. My husband has been enjoying our new home gym—and already has lost about 15 pounds. He and I are enjoying what can only be described as a *clutterless* relationship—spending more quality time together than ever before, working to create the lives we want.

Because we have embraced this process, our home is not just beautiful, well organized, and a restful place for us to connect with each other—it has become a sanctuary for others to become inspired to live unencumbered by the *too much*. We even shut off our cable TV. We are transformed. With less, thanks to you, we feel an overwhelming sense of gratitude, joy and abundance. I no longer fantasize about a place of my own—I'm too busy living the life I want, creating the home I want, doing the things that make me feel alive. We will continue to share your empowering message of hope with those in our circle. We feel blessed to have found you. We hold a special place in our hearts for you, Evan. Thank you. Thank you.

Hope

ZEN LIVING

I went to the woods because I wished to live deliberately, to front only the essential facts of life, and see if I could not learn what it had to teach, and not, when I came to die, discover that I had not lived. I did not wish to live what was not life, living is so dear; nor did I wish to practice resignation, unless it was quite necessary. I wanted to live deep and suck out all the

marrow of life, to live so sturdily and Spartan-like as to put to rout all that was not life, to cut a broad swath and shave close, to drive life into a corner, and reduce it to its lowest terms.
–Henry David Thoreau, Walden

There are those who seek to practice life reduced to its bare essence, stripped away of deceiving pageantry and flashy façade. They mark the pages of their days with meaningful experience, prized relationships, honest prose, and an uncommon perspective earned from pain and loss, redemption and peace. Stoic and humble among the noisy hubris of the masses, they seek the raw path of life, quietly guided by integrity of character and inspiration of purpose.

These genuine souls, though perhaps haunted by brazen circumstance, reveal a splintered glimpse of our full potential. *You know these people.* Their libraries are larger than their televisions. Their vision of reality is born along the ragged trail and high atop the summit peak. They know intimately the hearts and minds of those dearest to them. They seek understanding, stillness, and the simplicity of being. They do not always tread softly; often the impressions they leave are with indelible resolve. But they lead with compassion and generosity, for they understand empathy as a law of humanity.

Their material possessions offer little in the way of deep personal fulfillment. Like the master martial artist, the threadbare coveted belt is but a thing—whereas her knowledge and skill in spite of defeat holds tangible, substantive worth. Like monks and mountaineers, precious belongings offer simple, sentimental, artistic, and practical value. On the balancing scale of life, the fewer the possessions, the greater the sense of authentic abundance. The treasured things in their unencumbered spaces are carefully chosen, well-maintained, and mindfully revered on alters of memory and promise.

Their actions are deliberate. Thoughtfully executed with precision and poise, they honor the rhythms and cycles of nature, ebbing and flowing without judgment or pride. They strive to understand intricate complexity and thrive in the innovative discovery of efficient execution. Conservation in effort, energy, and resources are paramount to all action.

Their conceptual ideas blossom from cosmic vibration and deep emotions that churn to life from the slow blue flame of contemplation. Their ideas are calligraphy strokes of clarity with endless expression, transcending journey into wisdom, thought into purposeful action. They are not without blunder or folly—indeed, they are quite practiced at failure.

Above all else, these beautiful beings accidentally inspire the rest of us. They help us to sift through the relentless steaming piles of commercial bullshit for authentic experience, personal connection, and honest participation. They light up the darkness with enthusiasm, courage, and humor. They confidently lead with kindness—*sucking out all the marrow of life*. They do it *not* because of some physical prowess or intellectual advantage; but because they choose to. Despite all else, they simply *choose* to.

When we start with the uncompromising certainty that we are not what we possess or how we appear—but what and whom we love; when we radically accept ourselves as compassionate, contributing participants in an imperfect world; when we choose a life of substance with our perfect smiles, a little curiosity, and a dash of courage, we find that we are suddenly sucking down great big gobs of life in terrifically intoxicating gulps. Cheers to you—to a life lived with integrity and intention.

The greatest wealth is to live content with little.

– Plato

6
SERENITY OUT OF CHAOS

Dear Hope,

Once, when asked what surprised him most about human-ity, His Holiness the Dalai Lama answered, "Man. Because he sacrifices his health in order to make money. Then he sacrific-es money to recuperate his health. And then he is so anxious about the future that he does not enjoy the present; the result being that he does not live in the present or the future; he lives as if he is never going to die, and then dies having never really lived."

He has famously observed, "We have bigger houses, but small-er families; more conveniences, but less time; we have more degrees, but less sense; more knowledge, but less judgment; more experts, but more problems; more medicines, but less healthiness. We've been all the way to the moon and back, but have trouble crossing the street to meet a new neighbor. We built more computers to hold more information, to produce more copies than ever, but have less communication. We have become long on quantity, but short on quality. These are times of fast food, but slow digestion; tall men, but short character; steep profits, but shallow relationships. It is a time when there

131

is much in the window, but nothing in the room."

Hope, I am inspired by you and your family. I think we are young and an inherently complex species, and we make things harder than they need to be. It's not our fault. We're new to the cosmic circle of life, and we're still learning about synchronicity. I think, in general, the more we can live without, the easier it is to live a deeply rewarding life, unencumbered from things that distract us from why we are here—to live simply, inspired by love. The Dalai Lama says, "Our prime purpose in this life is to help others. And if you can't help them, at least don't hurt them." When we look at *how* we live through this lens, what we do serves this simple purpose. Everything else falls away, and all we're left with are the things that matter most: who we love, what we do, how and why we live—*because everything else is just stuff.* Thank you for sharing your journey with me, and with those in your life. Collectively, we can help create a new global paradigm: one that chooses simplicity, stewardship, compassion, generosity, sustainability, kindness, and love. It starts in our homes—but its reach is infinite. *This is our ClutterFree Revolution.*

Wishing you love and abundance,

Evan

I stumbled upon a key to unlock the doors that separate us from the life we seek. It's nothing complicated, a simple three step process designed for ease of use and universal application. Use it whenever you feel stuck. Teach it to your children.

IDEAL VISION

Ask yourself, "If I could create the best-case scenario, if I could wave my magic wand and have this already solved—what would it look like?" First, get a clear vision of where you'd like to end up, and then simply plot a course to get there. This is how:

STEP 1: SIMPLIFY

When looking at the stuff in your spaces, *start* with what you can get rid of. What can go away? Eliminating the volume of variables makes the process of managing the important stuff infinitely easier. When applying this method to complex concepts and theoretical ideas, simply replace the word "purge" with the word "focus." Everything else stays the same, but by concentrating your attention, energy, and effort, you will achieve hyper-focus on what matters most right now.

STEP 2: CLARIFY

Once you have purged that which is NOT essential, and achieved focus—it's time to get organized. Sort your *things* (and/or your information) using the Intentional Solutions' 4 Rules of Organization: 1) like things together, so items are 2) easy to find, 3) easy to reach, but 4) out of the way. Remember proximity = urgency explains how close something should be for imminent use or long-term storage. We'll need to conveniently access those things in order to leverage efficient operations and maximize effective use.

STEP 3: INSPIRE

Because everything that functions at peak performance requires maintenance, bring your space (or idea) to life with vibrancy and style. Ownership of what you have created through its 1) aesthetic, 2) function, 3) flexibility, and 4) customization to suit your personal lifestyle preferences, will inspire accountability to purposeful action. The systems you set up to maintain your ideal vision will help you achieve long-lasting results. Like getting into shape for the big race, training makes this work easier, more rewarding—and more fun.

NOW IT'S YOUR TURN

Think about a space and/or an idea where you feel STUCK.

Create Your Ideal Vision

Briefly write down your ideal vision for that space or how you would like to see that idea blossom into reality. When it comes to interior design, I recommend the Houzz app (www.Houzz.com), though there are countless other online and print platforms available to help inspire your ideal vision. Create your own vision, write a brief narrative, cut and paste photos and illustrations, or draw something that represents how you would like each of your spaces to look and feel. When we start with the end in mind, it becomes a virtual checklist of things to do.

Step 1: Simplify

What can you purge to make room for what your space is about to become? What can you eliminate in order to achieve hyper-focus on this idea?

Step 2: Clarify

What needs to be organized to help create clarity around the essential elements of this space/idea?

Step 3: Inspire

How can we bring this space/idea to life with style and vibrancy?

The answers to these questions become the things you must accomplish in order to reach the ideal vision you set first. Schedule these items into your calendar or day planner system, and follow through with intentional resolve. Integrity is doing what you say you will do. Clearing the cluttered path to the life you seek is as simple as setting the intention and taking incremental steps to reaching your goal.

Life happens. It will throw you curve balls and obstacles, so expect them. Plan for contingencies to help keep you going. Flexibility is a good thing, but ultimately, you control your own destiny. Wander some. Experience life outside your comfort zone. Try new things, just to see what else is out there. Become fearlessly curious about how to leverage who you want to be, and what you want to do.

Time is so short, and life is so fragile, so tread softly, love unapologetically, and commit to serving others as we serve ourselves. You'll get there. When you feel stuck, remember to come back to step one and ask yourself, "How can I simplify this?" If you feel like you're spinning your wheels, you're probably skipping steps, so go back to step one and *simplify*. Use it to manage your literal and figurative clutter whenever you feel stuck. Share it with your friends and teach it to your children.

My office had become the dumping room for everyone else's gear! Hockey, lacrosse, camping, hunting - EVERYTHING except the things I needed in my home office! Evan helped me to make sense of it all. Together, we went through everything and prioritized what to keep, toss, recycle, give away and store. Now, my beautiful, organized office has a floor, cleared shelves and a functional desk! It was a huge relief to get rid of the backlog of all that stuff - and take back some work space for myself! Yes, it was worth it and yes, Evan will be coming back again!
– Sophie Schlumberger

CLEAN YOUR ROOM, CHANGE YOUR LIFE: A CASE STUDY

DENISE LATOUSEK

In 2012 when I started my business, I was invited by two local newspapers to publish a column twice a month about my work. It's how many of my clients have come to find me. One of them was Denise Latousek.

Denise, a professional fitness instructor, her husband Michael, a reputable real-estate broker, and their daughter had finally moved into a new house after an exhausting series of temporary moves. Denise was pregnant with their second daughter when they finally moved into the home where they would stay until the girls went off to college. Hard as they tried to settle in, they hit a snag that brought everything to a screeching halt.

In the midst of all that moving around, Denise suffered a debilitating hip injury that left her physically and psychologically broken. Chronic complications led to multiple surgeries and more complications thwarted ongoing attempts at recovery. All of this was going on as they attempted to unpack and move into the new house. Denise's excruciating ordeal lasted about three years – and they never fully settled in.

Her physical recovery was slow, deliberate and emotionally painful. She discovered that perseverance was the primary ingredient to performance. It didn't matter how slowly she progressed, as long as she kept moving forward. It was that determination that brought her out of the ashes and back to a thriving career as a fitness professional in the most prestigious fitness centers of Aspen, Colorado. When she finally called me, her home felt unfinished and in too much disarray to give her the mental clarity she knew she needed to launch her own business.

After a few years, their spaces were chronically cluttered with stuff: toys, exercise equipment, photo albums, clothes and shoes for every season, work stuff, arts and crafts materials, sporting goods, household paperwork, electronics, home office stuff, and well – they had a lot of *stuff*. It was clear that their things had become a barrier to success, an undefined liability that was holding them back.

Denise called me looking for a few simple strategies to simplify their home and to help sort it all out. This was a typical client call for me. But I had no idea then how it would change Denise's life forever.

My work with Denise started in her basement, tidying up and refreshing a media room and a home gym. After one or two intense sessions with me, we migrated upstairs to the kids' playroom, which had not been used in a while because it was too cluttered. We re-established a fun space for the girls to play, created an arts and crafts corner, as well as a work station that has since become Denise's home office. After several visits, her husband Michael called me to help organize the garage. Over time, their home became utterly transformed, and they fell in love with the house all over again (for the first time since they moved in). The ongoing process of purging, organizing and refreshing their spaces became a staging ground for what would happen next.

My professional practice is focused in five areas: organization, operational systems, time and task management, content creation, and professional networking. Denise knew then that I could help her to take the next step towards clearing the cluttered path to the life she sought.

Only a few months after helping the Latouseks dial in their spaces, Denise called me asking for help with an idea to start her own business. Together, we started drafting a business plan, flushing out what she wanted to do – her ideal vision for where she wanted her business to go, and then we simplified it (**step 1: Simplify**). That is to say we purged all conflicting ideas that were either not viable, cost prohibitive, or not so interesting. Expert industry guru, Brendon Burchard, says "The main thing is to let the main thing be the main thing." So we got super focused on what her ideal business was and what it *wasn't*.

Once we had all the components of her business plan sketched out on paper, we needed clarity about what to do with each of them. That meant organizing every last detail of her plan (**step 2: Clarify**). With a little help from our shared professional network, we started a website, wrote copy, did market research, opened accounts, compiled financial projections, developed programming, created logos and got a handle on administrative details and legal logistics. We used Trello.com to organize the particulars (the free online project management platform designed for achieving effective clarity and communication). With Michael's connections in local real estate, he had already secured a potential lead on a beautifully renovated yoga studio in the downtown core, only blocks from their home. With the details in order, and the loan approved, Denise took the leap and signed the lease on her gorgeous new fitness studio within a matter of months.

Once she was in, things got a lot more fun with the creative design of the space and her company brand (**step 3: Inspire**). First we finalized her logo, polished up her website and preliminary collateral materials, and started submitting promotional notices. We took out public service announcements, started a Facebook page, launched a soft-opening campaign, and got a full-spread feature article in *The Aspen Times*. She was interviewed by the local television station that covers Aspen's hottest trends. Before she knew it, people were signing up for her newsletters, engaging on social media, and registering as members—all *before* she opened her doors. She remodeled the space, using contemporary furnishings that gave her studio a hip lounge vibe, complete with a state-of-the-art sound system and retail merchandising. By the time she opened, she had a highly-qualified team of fitness instructors, certified in the top-rated fitness programs. Her grand opening was less than nine months from the time we first met.

Remember, when Denise moved into her new home, her place

was a mess and she could not even walk! Today, Denise is founder and CEO of Burn Fitness Studio, one of the premier fitness centers of the Aspen Valley. She boasts a high-volume loyal following, and continues to roll-out the most internationally-acclaimed group fitness programs of our time. A gifted entrepreneur, with a talent for style and a commitment to unparalleled customer service, Denise has become somewhat of a local celebrity. She is widely respected for her rapid success and applauded for her commitment to serving her community with sincerity, integrity, and distinction. Not only that, she's now in the best shape of her life and specializes in fitness for injury recovery! She is a poster-child for what we can do when we clear out, clean up, and focus on what matters most.

We moved into a new home and never really unpacked. With two kids and a ton of stuff, after a few years it was time to clean out and get organized. How much is it worth to completely transform the cluttered, under-used rooms in your home into fun spaces that energize and inspire the entire family? Intentional Solutions is the real deal! Evan is fast, effective and inspiring. I finally have a functional home office, an organized creative arts studio, and a home gym. Evan's system is easy to understand and easy to apply right now—in any space, with dramatic results after every single session. Worth every penny! Evan's practical strategies have transformed my home, my business, and my life. You won't find comprehensive services this good anywhere. The best investment I've made.
—Denise Latousek

Denise's inspiring true story illustrates the power of rapid transformation when we get clarity about what matters most. *ClutterFree Revolution* is not just another how-to-organize book—it is a movement of forward-thinking people, committed to clearing the cluttered path to the lives we seek. Our spirit is inspired by an ideal vision for marvelous possibility. Our actions are informed by a certainty that *what we do matters*. We are thoughtful, confident, and driven by a unique calling to create our lives with intention, rather than surrender to the sheer momentum of circumstance.

This revolution is a community of believers, united in support of one another—in opposition to those who would see our dreams drowned in a sea of meaningless piles of stuff. We are intrinsically motivated to flourish—not by fashionable trends—but through our courage, resourcefulness, and determination. We understand that true democracy requires participation, and therefore we commit to purposeful action, in favor of ideas that support peace and sustainable life over grossly inflated profit margins for a small handful of bullies. We know that every revolution requires *boots on the ground*— activists willing to share what they know, speak out against tyranny, and fight for what is just. Individually, we see the opportunity to contribute to the collective good in the smallest acts of kindness. And little by little, we take steps towards one another.

Look at the cover of *this* book. If you are reading this, you probably have a pair of shoes you no longer wear. Think of the person out there right now—with almost nothing—no food, no shelter, no hope—cold, lonely, walking around barefoot. What steps can you take—right now—to clear *your* clutter and help another human being to improve the quality of their life? The ClutterFree Revolution is a movement to reallocate precious resources from those drowning in the *too much*, to those struggling to survive with so little. It is a movement to take personal responsibility for what we do every day in support of one another.

The Conscious Consumer's Manifesto

Conscious consumerism is a movement to revolutionize what we buy, why we buy it, and from whom. It inspires a curiosity about the origins of the goods we consume, and a commitment to ensuring those purchases support sustainable life. The result of this movement is not just good for us individually as consumers and collectively as members of the human race, it's also good for business and supports macro-ecosystems and economies on a global scale.

How do we become conscious consumers? First, we must simplify. We must look inward and discover that the intentional absence of excess creates the tangible space for abundance. We must cleanse ourselves and our homes of *the cheap, the toxic,* and *the too much,* for they are killing us—all of us. We must learn to value the virtues of being nimble, flexible, adaptable, and resourceful; virtues that come from a lifestyle that promotes peace and sustainable life—above profit.

In the midst of the information age where everything moves at the "speed of business," we have lost sight of what matters most. Yes, we are all hypocrites to one degree or another. But we must start somewhere. We must do what we can. Start locally. Shop second-hand. Rip out your grass and grow an organic garden. Invest in your own local community's ability to deliver goods and services. Boycott industries, stores, brands, and people that perpetuate the problem. Support the dreamers, idealists, and visionaries who support the revolution to a healthier, more peaceful, more sustainable future.

Relative to the vast majority of people in the world, first world luxuries afford us the flexibility, indeed the obligation, to consider how we might bring a little consciousness to the global solution. This is the *ClutterFree Revolution.*

What you do makes a difference and you have to decide what kind of difference you want to make.

—Jane Goodall

You never change things by fighting the existing reality. To change something, build a new model that makes the existing model obsolete.

– Buckminster Fuller

7
JOIN THE REVOLUTION

In the introduction, I stated:

This book is not about organizing your closets. It is a call to arms, a rally cry to take a stand in the revolution against Corporatocracy and commercial imperialism—to champion a new standard of common sense and sustainability. At its very core, the revolution starts in our homes, with our families. For those looking to evolve out of a cluttered existence, this book is a practical guide to inform, instruct, and inspire the journey to a better life—a more rewarding, more meaningful, more intentional life of purpose and abundance.

This book is about reprioritizing, redirecting scarce resources, developing a more sustainable paradigm of market accountability and consumer responsibility. If you are reading this, you probably have more opportunity and more viable resources than three quarters of the earth's population. Paring down our stuff and becoming mindful about our spaces is not just a pleasant alternative to living in disarray, it is a moral imperative as members of the human race. How we behave as consumers has profound implications on what happens at home and around the globe. This book is an instruction manual for a return to intentional simplicity, a return to less stuff and more life.

We live in an unprecedented time of instability. From ecological and environmental uncertainty to economic, social, and geopolitical volatility—humanity is at a dire crossroads. The burden of this tumultuous time falls on the shoulders of those struggling to survive the day, not those arrogantly counting their daily profits. Native American Cree elder, Alanis Obomsawin, is famously quoted as stating sadly, "Your people are driven by a terrible sense of deficiency. When the last tree is cut, the last fish is caught, and the last river is polluted; when to breathe the air is sickening, you will realize, too late, that wealth is not in bank accounts and that you can't eat money."

Every great civilization in history has fallen. Specifically, this happens when those in power strategically perpetuate instability. Their remarkable greed and unspeakable hubris undermined balance, equality, and opportunity for sustainability. Inevitably, the masses revolted, resources depleted—and perhaps the planet itself shook us off to begin anew. It's happening NOW. Wake up. Look around. SEE the conditions people and other creatures of this planet endure beyond your own neighborhood. Understand their pain, their conflict, their longing, their fight to exist. Connect the dots between how we live, with the impact we have on them.

CHAPTER SEVEN

*Any man's death diminishes me, because I am involved
in mankind, and therefore never send to know for
whom the bells tolls; it tolls for thee.*
– John Donne

Here is a wakeup call: among other things, our planet is running out of fresh water. Megacities around the globe are about to face unparalleled trials that will only get worse in the coming years. My friends, the effects of climate change and our exponentially increasing populations have stretched our capacity for survival beyond what is being reported on the nightly news. The media, the Food and Drug Administration, health care, elected officials—our own governments have been bought by corporate interests.

While science goes hoarse in their cries of warning, our leaders belittle the threat and encourage us to go shopping. We are about to see how fragile modern civilizations truly are. The next couple of decades will, in fact, illuminate how flimsy our paradigms of permanence have become—and the people of the world will realize, too late, what matters most.

The ClutterFree Revolution is not about tidying up. It's about opening our eyes, and individually taking responsibility for our unintended and careless actions. It's about standing up to those who seek to maintain the status quo; it's about collectively revolting against our inevitable demise. It's affirming that WHAT WE DO MATTERS and it starts with what we do with our own families in our own homes.

The ClutterFree Revolution is about empowering a generation of global citizens, united behind the conservation of precious life-giving resources in support of one another. It is about taking deliberate and purposeful action to support our species and the effective preservation of our planet. The effects of our voracious consumption have reached a terminal apex, one from which there is no going back. Unless we immediately shift our collective effort to sustainability, the viability of modern human survival will become as improbable as countless civilizations before us. The writing is on the wall; let us see it is as a call to action. Let us come to terms with our past, and unite in a common future. Let us raise our children in support of our very existence, in defiance of those few who would unapologetically step on our throats to protect their own assets and interests. Please—for the sake of our children—let us not waste this critical hour shopping for one more goddamn thing.

Let us recommit to stewardship, responsibility, innovation, and ingenuity. If we are to survive, let us reject commercialization and the toxic drivel relentlessly stuffed down our throats. Let us vote with our forks. Let us reach out to one another, united with the people of the world with our wallets, our ideas, and our energy in support of environmental conservation, practical minimalism, humanitarian philanthropy, organic food production—and common sense birth control. Let us return to realistic and practical strategies for survival on this planet, and not die the self-defeating zombies the ubiquitous few intend for us to become.

We don't need much to be happy. Choose a lifestyle of less, get organized and reprioritize your precious resources away from mindless consumerism, and collectively demand account- ability to those intentionally sabotaging our future. In other words, simplify your stuff. Vote with your fork, your wallet, and your bicycle. Need less. Starve the wolves at Monsanto, Big Oil, and the military-industrial complex and start feeding innovation, sustainability, and education. Whichever we feed will become our future.

Let me state clearly again: I'm not perfect. I'm just a man - plausibly a hypocrite. I am guilty of living comfortably in this modern age of economic and social disparity. Perhaps it is too late for us. As this book goes to print, my daughter is now five years old. I wish for her what I wish for all children, to have the opportunity to learn, grow, travel, create, innovate, love, and thrive, to start a family of her own. I wish for her to know a brighter future—with promising potential for unlimited to- morrows, in a world celebrating rich diversity and life-giving sustainability. I write this book for her—and for her genera- tion. I invite you to join me—and countless others across the globe, clinging to hope for our children. I invite you to shed your literal and figurative excess, embrace simplicity, nurture sustainability, and help clear the cluttered path to the life we all seek. Join the ClutterFree Revolution, take intentional ac- tion, and do your part to ensure tomorrow's promise is one of peace, love, and abundance.

*My mission in life is not merely to survive, but to thrive;
and to do so with some passion, some compassion,
some humor, and some style.*

– Maya Angelou

CLUTTER FREE ZEN MASTERY

I'd Like to Support You in Your Journey to Becoming a ClutterFree Zen Master.

Visit me online at **www.MyIntentionalSolutions.com** and learn about opportunities for working with me directly. As an organizational solutions and strategies consultant, I help people simplify so they can focus on what matters most, and that is: who we love, what we do, how and why we live, *because everything else is just stuff.* My professional practice is focused in 5 areas:

1. Organization
2. Operational Systems
3. Time & Task Management
4. Content Creation (Idea Development, Copy Writing, Business Development, Program Development, Curriculum Development, Professional and Career Development) and
5. Professional Networking.

I invite you to connect with me directly to find out how Intentional Solutions can help you clear the cluttered path to the life you seek. **Evan@MyIntentionalSolutions.com**

CLUTTER FREE
REVOLUTION™
ACADEMY
SIMPLIFY YOUR STUFF.   ORGANIZE YOUR LIFE.   SAVE THE WORLD.

SUPER TERRIFIC VERY SPECIAL ULTRA EXCLUSIVE BOOK OFFER

I'll be blunt: I'm not a big fan of impersonal freebies and generic book offers that try bribing me to sign up for something I don't need. That's just noise, and quite frankly, I'm not interested. For me, it's all about making meaningful connections with real people. Building relationships is my bottom line. It's how I was raised, how I built my business, and how this revolution will gain traction on a global scale. Millions of others like me are on a social crusade to help save the world. I'd like to support the effort by positioning myself to engage with those inspired individuals.

So, if you're interested, here's my super terrific, very special, ultra-exclusive book offer:

My professional practice is all about helping people to simplify – their homes, their stuff, their spaces, their families, and their lives. I started out working in and around Aspen, Colorado, but after honing my 3-Step Method with clients over time, I discovered that talking people through the process was just as effective as working with folks on-site. In fact, **I kept getting the same feedback from my clients: "I need your voice in my head, talking me through these steps**." So I created a companion program to the book, a supplemental curriculum to help anyone – anywhere. And all you need is a phone.

That program has evolved into what is now the **ClutterFree Revolution ACADEMY**™.

Offered only a few times every year, "**CFR ACADEMY**" is an interactive, 90-day deep dive immersion for those who love the content of the book, but want a little extra help doing the work in their own homes. Delivered simply via telephone and a private forum on Facebook, this three-month semester course offers a colossal amount of information and support, and is designed to be instructive, informative, and inspiring. Because the program is interactive, the content of *ClutterFree Revolution* becomes hyper-focused on YOU.

More comprehensive than anything you are likely to find elsewhere, the unique **CFR ACADEMY program includes**:

✓ **12 Weeks of LIVE Teleconferencing** with Bestselling Author and Organizational Expert, Evan Michael Zislis

✓ **Two 1-Hour Group Calls Every Week for Three Months**, Covering a New Module & a Follow-Up Q&A Call Twice Every Week

✓ **Multiple Opportunities to Call In Every Week** + Downloadable Recordings of Every Call for Your Scheduling Convenience

✓ **Comprehensive Downloadable Curriculum Guide** to Cover Every Facet of Simplifying & Organizing Every Room of Your Home

✓ **Free PDF of the Amazon Bestselling eBook,** *ClutterFree Revolution*

✓ **Lifetime Membership to the CFR ACADEMY Mastermind** Group Hosted on a Private Forum on Facebook, including:

- Weekly Updates for Recommended Links, Additional Resources and Inspirational Solutions
- Weekly Before & After Pictures Posted by Other Students and the Members of the CFR **ACADEMY** Mastermind
- Live Chat with CFR **ACADEMY** Host, Evan Michael Zislis, and Other Members of the CFR **ACADEMY** Mastermind Group
- 24/7 Access to All New, Revised and Upgraded Curriculum Materials for the Life of the CFR **ACADEMY** Program
✓ **Surprise Gifts & Bonuses TBD**

If you are ready to simplify your stuff, organize your life— and save the world, the CFR ACADEMY is for YOU.

As my **personal gift** for investing in this program and committing to the ClutterFree Revolution, it would be my great pleasure to offer you a FREE autographed copy of my book, *ClutterFree Revolution*. Keep it for yourself or share it with someone you love.

CFR **ACADEMY** is only offered three times every year and enrollment is limited. To learn more and secure your spot for the upcoming semester, please visit our website at: www.ClutterFreeRevolution.com.

Wishing you love and abundance,

"Let the beauty of what you love be what you do."

–Rumi

MEET THE AUTHOR

Evan Michael Zislis is founder of the strategies consulting firm, Intentional Solutions, and author of *The Aspen Times* column *Life. Simplified.* The son of an Army pathologist, Evan discovered the virtues of simplicity during his youth. Traversing the planet every twenty minutes or so, Evan learned the Zen of simplifying, staying organized, and refreshing new spaces—over and over again.

With a master's degree focused in curriculum development and experiential education, Evan began his career as an educator, teaching 7th grade social studies at Aspen Middle School in Aspen, Colorado. He went on to enjoy a dozen years in nonprofit program development and organizational leadership before launching his own business in 2012.

Inspired by conscious consumerism, environmental conservation, and experiential education, Evan founded Intentional Solutions, a unique strategies consulting firm designed to help people simplify, so they can focus on what matters most: who we love, what we do, how and why we live; *because everything else is just stuff.* Intentional Solutions' proven-effective services span five primary areas: 1) organization, 2) operations,

3) time and task management, 4) content creation, and 5) professional networking.

Evan's touchstone, the Intentional Solutions 3-Step Method (Simplify, Clarify, Inspire), offers a timeless and universal framework for helping people to manage clutter, both literal and figurative—in all areas of life. Working with clients locally, nationally, and abroad, his professional practice delivers on-site, hands-on, practical strategies designed to help people simplify, get organized, and inspire long-lasting results.

Evan works with households, businesses, students, and people in life transition.

He lives with his family in Carbondale, Colorado.

CPSIA information can be obtained at www.ICGtesting.com
Printed in the USA
LVOW07s0042130116

470369LV00014B/484/P